HOW TO
ADULT

A guide to not being
a trash human,
and other life lessons

ANNA BLACKIE

LOST
THE
PLOT

LOST
THE
PLOT

A Lost the Plot Book, first published in 2020 by Pantera Press Pty Limited
www.PanteraPress.com

Please send all permission queries to:
Pantera Press, P.O. Box 1989 Neutral Bay, NSW, Australia 2089 or info@PanteraPress.com

A Cataloguing-in-Publication entry for this book is available from the National Library of Australia.

ISBN 978-1-925700-39-8

Cover and Internal Design: Elysia Clapin
Illustrations: Alex Nicol/@perceptioninfection
Publisher: Martin Green
Editor: Lucy Bell
Proofreader: Cristina Briones
Author Photo: Lucy Bell
Printed and bound in China by Shenzhen Jinhao Color Printing Co., Ltd

Pantera Press policy is to use papers that are natural, renewable and recyclable products made from wood grown in sustainable forests. The logging and manufacturing processes are expected to conform to the environmental regulations of the country of origin.

For Mum and Dad.

Thanks for giving me life
and teaching me to adult.

Sorry about all the swearing...

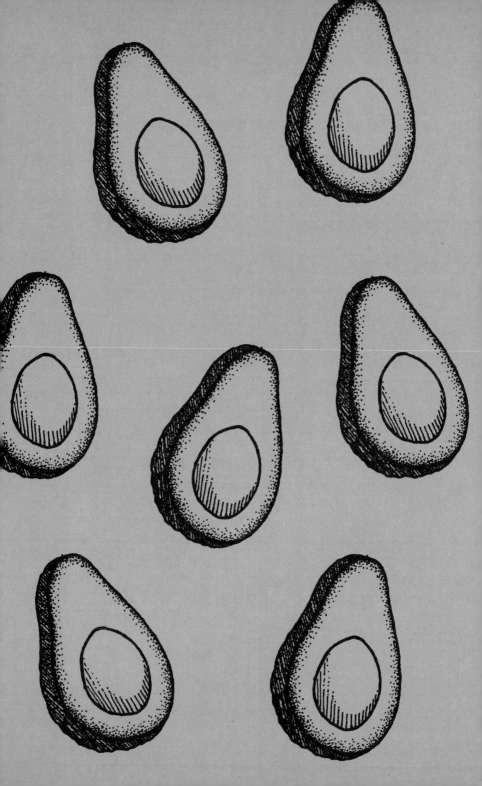

CONTENTS

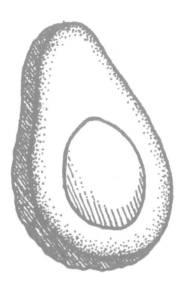

WELCOME TO THE TERRIFYING ADULT WORLD

Adulting. It's hard and stupid, and to be completely honest with you, I'd rather not do it. But the unfortunate truth of the matter is at some point, no matter how adamantly we try to deny it, adult responsibilities are coming for us all. As an avocado-toast-loving millennial, I find the concept of no longer calling my mum for every minor life inconvenience daunting and disorientating. How am I meant to survive in this frightening world of taxes, booking doctors' appointments and ironing without the sage and grumpy wisdom of the generation that came before? It feels like there's an awful lot of shit I should know, and the window for learning it seems to have come and gone.

Herein lies the idea behind *How to Adult*. In an attempt to appear as if I have my shit together, it seemed wise to collate all the menial and seemingly simple tasks and knowledge that had somehow passed me by, to guide both myself and my fellow hopeless millennials towards a greater future! Together, we'll learn how to make delicious sauces that will fool people into thinking your diet consists of more than mac and cheese, how to escape your problems by climbing a tree, the mysteries of the peach-butt, how to pretend you know about superannuation and taxes, and why you always need a fully stocked first-aid kit.

In a bleak reflection of my cluster-fuck of a life, the information in this guidebook is a compilation of research and interviews. Incredibly smart and knowledgeable people have been forced to sit down and spew their infinite knowledge of finite topics into my tiny brain so that I, in turn, can enlighten and inform all of you. If learning to do things that you should probably already know how to do is something that appeals to you, then read on, get wise and grow the fuck up.

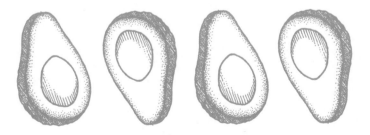

MONEY
IS SCARY AND
HERE'S
WHY

BEFORE WE DELVE into the scary world of financial-things-you-should-understand-but-probably-don't, there's one glaring take-home message for us all: if you want to do well financially, you have to pay attention to, and be engaged with, your money. I know, I know, this finance shit is super stressful and intense, and I've spent the majority of my life trying to pretend that money is a thing that only needs to be dealt with when you're old and have to feed your children/ herd of cats. But, as it turns out, money is a massive fucking deal to everyone, forever. There's no escaping it, even when you die. Did you know funerals are really expensive? Me neither, and now I have anxiety about the price of my coffin…

As an avoidant millennial terrified by the worrying state of their own finances, I approached a knowledgeable accountant/grown-up to assist me in understanding this mind-boggling financial world, and maybe even tell me how to make some free money.*

*Free money-making advice not included.

DEATH > TAXES

US Founding Father Benjamin Franklin once said that there are only two certainties in the world: death and taxes. Unfortunately for us, the latter is extraordinarily persistent, and in all truth will probably make you pray for the former. For those of you who are blissfully unaware, every time you're paid, a portion of your income is deducted for tax. These taxes are used by the government for health, education, defence, roads and railways – all the big important things that make our society tick. The amount you pay in tax is calculated based on your income. At the end of the financial year (that's June 30 for those of you living under a rock), everyone with an income is required to submit a tax return. These days, tax returns are submitted online, and include your overall income from work or investments, as well as any work-related expenses.

As with most things financial (and adult), the key to doing your taxes well is organisation. Even the best accountant can only do so much with limited information. Keeping orderly records makes the heinous process of lodging your tax return a million times easier, not to mention there's a chance you can claim on a whole mess of shit, which is essentially the government compensating you for the frustrating task of having to deal with your taxes to begin with…

The following documents and information are essential ingredients for tax time.

RECEIPTS

Stuff them in a folder and worry about them at the EOFY. If you're feeling extra organised and adulty, photograph your receipts and email them to yourself, then save them in an 'Invoices 2019' or 'I really hope I can claim these unnecessary expenses' folder for when tax time comes around.

The Australian Taxation Office has a handy overview of what can and can't be claimed for most jobs, but if you're unsure, keep as much as possible and ask a financial guru for assistance and pray that all the things you've wasted your money on in the last year are deemed worthwhile. A good rule of thumb is that anything that

Let your inner hoarder rejoice. Taxes are the perfect excuse to hold on to all those random receipts you don't know what to do with.

has contributed to your work can be claimed. For example, if you're a designer and you need to buy a subscription to Photoshop, that's an essential work expense. Similarly, if you work at McDonald's and have to buy a uniform, that too can be claimed.

GROUP CERTIFICATE OR PAYG PAYMENT SUMMARY

At the end of each financial year, your employer will provide you with a summary of how much you were paid that year, complete with a depressing overview of how much of your gross payments went to tax – joy! This summary is known as a group certificate or Pay As You Go (PAYG) payment summary. If you work multiple jobs, you'll receive a payment summary from each of your employers, and you will need to include all of these in your tax return.

PERSONAL INFO

Ideally, at this point in your life you'll actually know most of your personal details – however, I'm not overly confident in your life abilities, so I'm going to assume the worst. With everything tax and income, there are really only two things you need: your tax file number (TFN) and bank details.

IMPORTANT INFORMATION OR ABSOLUTE TRASH?

Where is the line between being organised and being a hoarder? Where does the separation between keeping documents 'for your records' meld into being a trash person who can't leave their house because they're trapped under a sea of old grocery receipts? These are some of the most enduring questions of my adulthood…

For tax purposes, there is a general rule for how long you should keep those scraps of paper that line the bottom of your bag.

1 month	Purchase and withdrawal receipts: Purchase receipts are a record of sale in the form of a tax invoice and can be both work-related and personal.
1 year	Pay slips and medical receipts.
7 years	Receipts for any tax deductions, including donation and work-related expenses.

There are some things that should be kept forever, so file this shit away in a little box for someone else to deal with when you die.

* **Birth certificate**
* **Citizenship papers**
* **Divorce certificates**
* **Passport**
* **Power of attorney**
* **Will**
* **Investment records:** home-purchase receipts, stock records, jewellery receipts and valuations
* **Tax returns**

BUDGETING: BECAUSE LOTTO TICKETS ARE NOT A FINANCIAL PLAN

To put together a budget, you need to have a good idea of what your incoming earnings and outgoing costs are. One of the phrases that makes accountants hate their jobs more than they already do is: 'I just don't know where all my money goes'. It's a sentiment I've expressed every day of my life, and it's fairly counterintuitive to budgeting or saving. At the end of the day, you can put together the best budget in the world, but if you're not counting the 15 drinks and late-night pizza you pretend not to buy every Saturday night, it's not going to do anything for you. So, before you start a budget, here are a few simple tips to get yourself in order.

START AN EXPENSE DIARY

Having an accurate idea of what you're spending, and when, is the foundation of building a budget that will work for you. You don't have to use a physical diary – these days, fancy online banking apps will chart your expenses and even categorise them, so you know what portion of your money is going to leisure, dining, unnecessary purchases and essentials like the sea of avocado toast you need to fuel your poor financial decisions.

ACCOUNTABILITY FOR LONG-TERM EXPENSES

We all have those shitty expenses that only crop up quarterly or annually that we completely forget about until they decimate our bank accounts, leaving us broke and crying in the corner. Making note of when your car registration, insurance, or loan repayments are due will make it a lot easier to calculate your total yearly income and outgoing costs and avoid the swirling void of debt and depression.

WHAT ARE YOUR LONG-TERM SAVING GOALS?

It might sound like a super simple strategy, but having a mental image of that thing you're desperately saving for every time you go to buy something unnecessary is one of the most foolproof ways to manage your spending. Just think of that ridiculously decadent holiday to Ibiza when you're buying a kebab with the lot after a night out, and let the subsequent spending guilt ensue. Naming your bank accounts with whatever it is you're saving for is the perfect way to keep those goals in mind. Every time you deposit into your 'Ibiza Holiday' account, you're one step closer to shirking your adult responsibilities.

LET OTHER PEOPLE DO THE BORING STUFF

As it turns out, everyone is bad at budgeting. But there are a few elite geniuses who capitalise on our global epidemic of poor financial planning, and provide the financially-challenged masses with a surplus of budgeting templates and apps. Rather than undergo the tedious project of creating your own budget, steal from the hive-mind that is the internet. Two examples are:

* The Pineapple Project
* Mint (app)

WTF IS DEBT AND HOW NOT TO USE A CREDIT CARD

The horrific freefall into adulthood brings with it a bevy of terrifying new frontiers: having to book doctors' appointments by yourself, buying your own birthday presents for family members, and the horrifying world of debt. For most of us, our first experience with debt comes from HECS (Higher Education Contribution Scheme). Fortunately (and unfortunately) for everyone with a worthless piece of paper framed on their wall, HECS is the type of debt that lives in the far-off 'I'll deal with it when I'm old' reality. HECS has given the low-income BA students of the world unrealistic expectations as to what debt actually is and how it affects us.

Put simply, debt is just owed money. It's generally the result of a loan, or a credit card after you've used it to make a big purchase that would make your normal bank account poop itself. These debts need to be repaid, usually with interest. In theory, loans and credit cards are great tools if you have a solid payment strategy in place. Well, that's the theory anyway… Without a repayment plan, loans and credit cards can easily cast you into the scary debt world.

Credit cards are the actual devil and should not be trusted.

MAGICAL MONEY CARDS

When I was younger and full of whimsical ignorance, I thought a credit card was a magical key to the hole in the wall filled with unlimited cash. My puny brain was under the impression that credit cards meant free money, and as far as I'm concerned, that's all anyone really wants in life. Now, after watching a substantial number of friends slip into credit-card debt, I've come to the sad realisation that free money doesn't exist. If you're wiser than me (which, let's face it, wouldn't be hard), you've probably already figured out some basic strategies to managing your credit card (or even how to avoid using it altogether). If not, learn from my mistakes.

* **Before you even get a credit card,** ask yourself if you actually need one – what will you be using it for, and how much will having access to credit impact your quality of life?

* **Have a look at your track record** for how you've been managing your money so far.

* **Is the card just for emergencies?** Like *actual* emergencies, not buying that pair of boots you desperately want just because they're on sale and they look cute AF and fit like a dream.

* **Understand the difference** between credit and debit: if you're using debit, you're paying for things with real money; with credit, you're borrowing from the bank to make your purchases – and those greedy arseholes are going to want their money back, plus interest…

* **Know the limit on your card,** and work out how long it would take you to pay it off if you reached that limit. A credit card works best when you can pay it off in full each month; that way, you avoid any interest charges, and you're basically using it as a next-level debit card.

If you can't pay off your credit card every month, pay it down as fast as possible. This may mean not saving anything for a few months, but it also means you avoid accumulating high-interest-rate charges.

GOOD INTEREST VS BAD INTEREST

Maths is hard, money is hard, and the only way I can understand these confusing financial things is to dumb them down as much as humanly possible. The way I have come to understand interest is by looking at it from two angles: there is the 'good' interest that helps you grow your money, and the 'bad' interest that takes that money away.

Good interest is generally associated with your savings account. Generally, a regular debit account won't have any interest applied to it, so if you want to make money with your money, the easiest way is to move it into a high-interest savings account or term deposit. Think of these accounts as little rooms for your money to make money babies, and then those babies have more babies until you have a room full of new money babies. Not my best analogy, but you get the picture.

Good interest is basically free money, which is my favourite free thing, closely followed by free food and alcohol.

On the other side of the spectrum, bad interest is the interest that robs you of your hard-earned money babies and leaves you bruised and battered on the floor. Bad interest comes from those dangerous loans and credit cards we covered earlier. On a credit card, interest is charged on the amount owed at the end of your predetermined interest-free period.

The amount charged is subject to your interest rate, which is why it's ridiculously important to know what your interest rate is before signing up for a credit card. As for loans, the interest rate and charge period varies depending on what type of loan you take out and which bank it's from.

Compound interest is a type of interest that gets charged on top of the interest you're already paying. Money is confusing and everything is terrifying.

Shit you should know

It's worth noting that the interest rate on loans and credit cards can also vary. Every so often, banks decide they want to charge more or less for loaning you money, when really they should just cut out the middleman and give us the money for free. But banks are greedy and we are poor… Such is life.

SUPER SENILITY SAVINGS

Superannuation is a government-organised system where a portion of your income is deposited into an account in preparation for the onset of your extreme old age, aka your retirement. It's basically the government's strategy to ensure the entire aged population doesn't end up on welfare. Unlike those other financial obligations we put off until we're old in the hope they'll just work themselves out, you don't have a choice: super is compulsory for anyone with an income.

For people employed by a company or organisation, the majority of their super maintenance is done by their employer. Once you start working, you establish your own super account with your chosen fund. This is one of those unfortunate adult things where you actually have to make an informed decision. Ew…

The $43,538 per year you need to stay alive once you retire is enough to buy 478 bottles of the fanciest vodka in my local bottle shop. Fuck being financially secure in your old age; live while you can!

There's a shit-ton of funds to choose from, and a whole bunch of things you should consider before committing to one.

✳   **Their fees:** Fees live to steal your hard-earned cash, and like taxes, are one of those seldom-talked-about downsides of financial maturity. The lower the fees on a super fund, the better. Make sure what you're paying is in line with (or below!) the industry standard. It also doesn't hurt to understand what the fees you're paying are doing; if you have a $400-per-month dickhead fee attached to your fund, you should probably look for something new.

✳   **Investment options:** A super fund works by investing your money into other things on your behalf. Depending on your fund, your super can be invested in a big range of crap, and this is where understanding who you fund and what they do is essential. What do they invest in? Is it something you agree with? If you're a diligent environmentalist, it's definitely worthwhile to invest in an ethical super fund that won't be feeding your cash into coal mining... There's also the high-risk and low-risk side of super investments. Some funds make investment decisions that are riskier than others, and while these funds can have a higher return it also means they can have bigger losses if it all goes pear-shaped.

✳   **It's all about performance:** Comparing which funds are performing best is a pretty important aspect of making that big, scary informed decision we've all been trying not to think about. Super plays the long game, so you need to take into account the last five years of performance history to get a proper idea of how they're going to handle your money over your working life.

Once you've chosen the super fund you want your money to live in, your employer starts making regular contributions from your pay. As of 2018, the superannuation rate was set at 9.5% of your overall income.

If you're self-employed, the responsibility of super contributions falls on you. Instead of following the 9.5% rate, you can determine how much – if any – of your income you want to set aside for your super.

The older you get, the more it makes sense to contribute to your own super, in addition to managing your own savings and investments in preparation for your oncoming senility... There are some nifty online calculators that figure out just how much money you'll need to keep you afloat once you retire – and prepare yourself: this shit is about to get depressing. For a 'comfortable lifestyle' it's estimated that you'll need around $43,538 per annum, this figure of course being dependent on how long you plan to live after you retire... With that in mind, I recommend as short a time as possible. That amount also doesn't take into consideration whether you were prepared enough, rich enough, or lucky enough, to own your home, have a partner, have kids or any of the other millions of terrifying adult-y variables that affect your financial situation.

While super is a compulsory thing that your employer is consistently contributing to (or you are managing yourself if you're self-employed), it is just one of several strategies you need to apply to prepare yourself for your retirement.

WHAT THE FUCK IS AN ACCOUNTANT, AND DO I NEED ONE?

It's a consistently baffling and terrifying life realisation that there are people out there, living in the world, who know how to do all the strange and scary things I have spent most of my life avoiding. Money? Finances? ADULT RESPONSIBILITY? No, thank you.

Luckily, accountants exist to pull us from the unending shame and dread spiral that we fall into at any mention of doing taxes. Accountants are creatures far smarter than you or me, whose job it is to maintain and inspect finances. They're better with your money than you'll ever be, so don't even try.

For all of you wondering if you need an accountant, the answer is twofold. If you don't have any assets, like a house, shares or investments of any kind, then you don't really need an accountant on retainer, which is a fee rich people pay to keep an accountant, or lawyer, around to provide their wisdom and guidance on a regular basis. All they

If you hire an accountant, they might help you save enough money to be rich enough to afford an accountant.

would do is tell you to stop spending your money on fancy coffees and excessive quantities of alcohol, and I don't know about you, but I came here to have a good time and I'm feeling super judged right now.

Accountants don't need to be hired on a permanent basis, and if you're as pathetic and hopeless as I am, they can be pretty useful when doing your tax return. While you still need to collect your receipts, an accountant can explain all the places you've gone wrong in your life, what you can and can't claim, and do all the shitty administrative aspects of your tax return for you – they're basically financial wizards. And although my unwillingness to part with what little money I have is a general deterrent to paying for anything, as it turns out, the fee you pay an accountant can be claimed in your following year of taxes. Not to mention, hiring one is pretty much an assurance that you're not going to fuck your tax up and have to pay the government for your stupidity.

Reasons why you should get an accountant:

* *They'll get you some sweet tax write-offs.*
* *They actually like math, so you're doing them a favour by asking them to do jobs you hate.*
* *They can improve your cashflow, meaning more dollars for you.*
* *If you own a business, they can help you eliminate unnecessary costs and measure your performance.*
* *When you fuck up your tax, the government gets mad; if an accountant fucks up your tax, you can feign ignorance and blame it all on them.*

Shit you should know

Now, I'm an avoidant millennial who's afraid to look at their bank account and thinks buying lotto tickets is a sustainable financial plan, so I'm not going to pretend to be the Barefoot Investor and try to give you guidance on any long-term or beneficial financial plans or investments. This is another instance where it might be advisable to seek out an accountant. In addition to being tax gurus, accountants are worth visiting if you're looking to invest money in shares or a house, or you're about to go through a big life change that's going to affect your financial situation, like getting married or having a kid (ew).

In short, if you're hopeless enough to need this book, then chances are you're too poor to need a long-term accountant. But having one you visit once a year to help you with your taxes is a sure-fire way to get you on track for some adult financial goals, and kill the stress that's been giving you premature greys.

I HAVE TOO MUCH MONEY, NOW WHAT?

Up until this point in my short and disastrous life, my strategy for dealing with a money surplus in my bank account has been to venture out into the world and spend it on anything exorbitant, alcoholic, or bad for me. Oddly, the older I get, the more I'm starting to realise this may not actually be a viable life plan. This is where investing comes in. Aside from having a kid, investing seems like one of the most adult things you can do. When you're still too juvenile to procreate, investing is the next best option. For those of you who have just been pretending to understand what you're reading so far, investing is when you put your bags of excess money into a financial scheme, like shares, stocks, bonds, mutual funds, exchange-traded funds and real estate (don't ask me what most of those are; again, my greatest investment so far has been in the degradation of my liver).

> Investing is just a sneaky way of saying you're buying a lot of fancy shit that you might want to sell later.

Recently two of my friends invested in a house together, making my most immature buddies absolute beacons of the adult lifestyle and poster boys for good decision-making. Watching their house-buying journey has shown me that buying property, as an investment or otherwise, is not as easy as walking into an open home and saying, 'I'll take this one'. In fact, it's a long and tedious process in which accountants, solicitors, property managers, bank contacts, credit unions and mortgage brokers all need to be consulted to ensure you're getting the best deal, signing the right contracts and succeeding as an adult with a diversified portfolio, plans and future prospects.

Shit you should know

Credit rating: *A credit rating (also known as a credit score) is a fun little number based on a composite of all your bad financial history (like unpaid debts and overdue credit card payments) and your good financial history (like assets and bills paid on time). Your credit rating is an indication of how financially trustworthy you are, and the higher your score the better. Credit scores really only come into play when you're looking to secure a loan from a bank or lender, where they use your score to determine whether you're worth the financial risk.*

As anyone with a brain would have gathered by now, I am not a wealth of knowledge when it comes to finances. Although I'm slightly the wiser for having written this book, I'm still terrified of that sad little pile of money I've been hoarding like some kind of Gringotts goblin for the last ten years. My future financial plans extend to the point of asking my dad

Creating money babies is far less physically strenuous than creating actual babies.

what to do, and then hoping I'll find a pot of gold at the bottom of a rainbow. Now that you're assured of my financial capabilities, I will leave you with some pearls of wisdom that sum up the entirety of all my investment know-how (I promise I asked an accountant about this).

✳   **Don't put all your eggs** in one basket. Having a diverse investment portfolio will help ensure you won't have huge losses in the long term if one of your investments falls through.

✳   'Take care of the cents and the dollars will look after themselves.' Exceptionally wise words from my grandmother, bestowed on me every time I turned my nose up at a five-cent piece. Translation: all money is good money; save it all, even if it means ditching your $5 almond lattes with a shot of vanilla syrup.

✳   **If you're investing in property**, pay attention to the location. Even if it's an investment you don't plan to live in, the location is just as important as the house itself.

✳   'Never invest in anything that flies, floats or foams.' The choice phrase of a distant uncle, and something I'm still trying to wrap my head around. Good luck with that.

✳   'Bring on another thousand.' The BOAT acronym, described to me by the father of an ex-boyfriend with lucrative funds and a bad history of boats running aground. Most of my financial wisdom comes from old people with a lot more money than me…

✳   'Someone's sitting in the shade today because someone planted a tree a long time ago.' This cringe-worthy quote from American billionaire Warren Buffett is actually wisdom worth listening to. One of the (many) reasons I've struggled to successfully grasp the concept of investing is because I am a sucker for instant gratification. Investment is all about developing something over the long term and preparing yourself for the future. This totally goes against the 'live fast, die young, leave a hot corpse' mentality I have been living by, but it's probably a better method for building a sustainable life. Seems like a lot less fun, though…

INCOME PROTECTION INSURANCE: IS MY $5 WORTH IT?

Life isn't all sunshine and rainbows. Shitty stuff happens like 85% of the time, and if you live a life of pessimism and despair like I do, you'll know that preparing for the worst is a necessity. That's where income-protection insurance comes in. This is an insurance policy that covers you if you were to get sick or injured and, as a result, be unable to work.

Like all insurance, you don't need it until you really need it. There's no halfway point. In reality, the people who most need income-protection insurance are those who are self-employed or have a gaggle of loud unruly children to look after. If you're a single 20-something with no kids, debt or pressing financial obligations, you can get away without being covered for the time being. But the moment you become the main breadwinner for a household with a mortgage and kids, it's probably time to consider insurance, or death. Both are viable options...

Shit you should know

Income protection might not be for everyone, and the idea of putting aside money for your savings every pay might seem like a ridiculously adult concept, but if there's one thing we've learnt from this adult world, it's that when it rains it pours. With that depressing adage in mind, it's always wise to have an emergency reserve of money at hand for an oncoming flash flood. Set aside enough money to cover a few weeks of your regular spending, so if you break your leg, get fired, or simply can't be fucked to do this whole nine-to-five thing a second longer, you won't be forced to sell off your worldly possessions and stand on your parents' doorstep begging them to take you in lest you live in a box on a street corner and die of hypothermia.

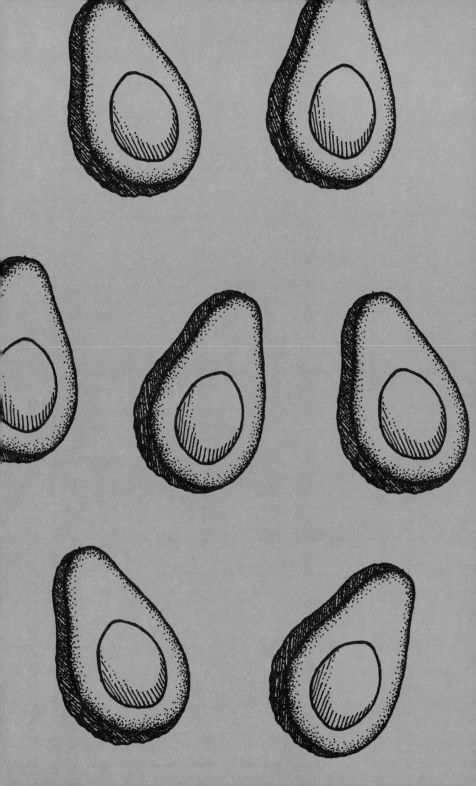

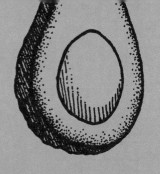
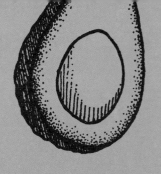

CULINARY
SKILLS
TO KEEP
YOU FROM
STARVATION

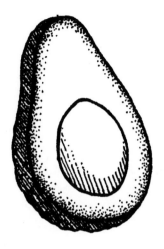

THERE'S A STRANGE SENSE of superiority that can be felt when one can accomplish simple kitchen tasks without having to call their mother five times in the process. The purpose of this chapter is to aid those who are culinarily challenged with a series of basic skills and some fundamental kitchen knowledge that is sure to fool your friends and family into thinking, *Wow, that young adult really has their life together.*

LET'S HAVE A SAUCY TIME

ROUx

Although it's not technically a sauce, roux is the cornerstone to many delicious kitchen endeavours. A mix of fat and flour, roux is essentially the base or thickening agent for a whole range of sauces, soups, stews and gravies.

There are two types of roux: a white and a blond. White roux is used to thicken milk-based sauces and dishes like béchamel, macaroni and cheese, tuna mornay and chowder. Blond or golden roux is used to create a richer, nuttier flavour as well as thicken a dish. This roux is commonly found in gravies and stews.

What You'll Need

Equal parts:

FAT, such as butter, vegetable oils, bacon drippings or lard

FLOUR

A good guideline is 2 tablespoons of the wet ingredient and 4 of the dry.

1 Heat your chosen fat on the stovetop over medium–low heat and add flour. Mix until smooth.

2 For white roux, stir over heat for several minutes to cook out the flour taste, then remove from heat.

3 For blond roux, keep on heat for around 20 minutes, stirring consistently to ensure the mixture doesn't burn. Your roux should turn a golden colour and have a toasted smell.

BÉCHAMEL

Béchamel, also known as white sauce or cheese sauce, is an important foundation to any lasagne, the delicious glue to a good fondue, or just a generally good time for anyone who wants to cover their food in a rich and decadent cheesy sauce.

Now you've learned how to make roux, you're ready to take the next step into culinary brilliance and prepare your béchamel.

What You'll Need

WHITE ROUX made with 60 g butter and ⅓ cup flour

2 CUPS MILK

70 G GRATED PARMESAN

50 G SHREDDED TASTY CHEESE

N.B. These are the perfect quantities for one deliciously cheesy family-sized lasagne.

1 Start with a white roux. Once this is ready, take off the heat and begin adding milk.

2 Add milk slowly in ½ cup increments, whisking constantly as you pour it into the roux.

3 Once milk is combined, return mixture to the heat and cook for 10 minutes, until sauce comes to the boil.

4 Add parmesan and tasty cheese and stir until combined.

5 Remove from heat and season to taste.

Shit you should Know

As a culinary genius and millennial who likes to live life on the wild side, I generally do my measurements by eye. For a good roux consistency, melt your desired amount of butter, and add flour until the mixture resembles fat golden breadcrumbs, then you're ready to add milk. Keep adding milk in parts until you have a thick sauce that smoothly coats the back of a spoon.

If this impromptu eyeballing method is just too crazy for you, remember these handy ratios so you never have to do any experimentation:

* ✳   *60 g butter, ⅓ cup flour, 2 cups milk*
* ✳   *1 tablespoon butter, 2 tablespoons flour, 1 cup milk*

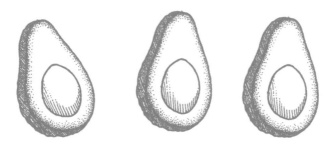

GRAVY

Gravy: the staple of every roast dinner and arguably the most important sauce you'll ever make. Real gravy is best prepared in addition to a delicious roast dinner; the fatty, liquid base of your gravy should ideally come straight from the baking tray of whatever succulent hunk of meat you've got waiting.

What You'll Need

THE ROAST *that will accompany your delicious sauce*

2 TABLESPOONS FLOUR

WATER: *start with a cup, but the amount you use will depend on your preferred thickness*

SALT AND PEPPER

1   When your roast has finished cooking, let it rest in the baking tray for about 10–15 minutes. Once it has cooled and all those sweet juices have found their way into the tray, remove the meat and transfer the fatty juices into a saucepan.

2   Put the pan on a low heat and allow liquid to bubble. Add flour (adjust amount depending on how much fat is in your pan) until a paste-like consistency forms. Stir for several minutes to cook out the flour taste.

3   Begin adding water in small portions. Let the gravy simmer as you mix until sauce reaches your ideal consistency.

4   Add salt and pepper to season, or follow the sage advice of Paul Kelly and add a dollop of tomato sauce for that extra tang. Alternatively, you can season with stock powder, soy sauce or Vegemite – we all know that anyone who says they don't like Vegemite is a damn liar; believe me, it adds a salty, rich flavour to the gravy. Delightful!

CHEATS' GRAVY

If you're craving a gravy but lacking the accompanying roast, there is a solution!

What You'll Need

50 G BUTTER

1 ONION, FINELY CHOPPED

2 CLOVES GARLIC

1 TEASPOON DRIED THYME

1 TEASPOON DRIED ROSEMARY

2 TABLESPOONS FLOUR

1½ CUPS EITHER CHICKEN, BEEF OR VEGETABLE STOCK

1   Melt butter in a saucepan over medium heat, then add onion.

2   As the onion cooks, add garlic, thyme and rosemary. Cook until onion is browned.

3   Add flour and stir.

4   In parts, slowly add stock. Bring gravy to the boil and stir for about 5 minutes then taste. If a floury flavour remains, continue stirring on heat for another 2–3 minutes.

5   Strain gravy into a serving jug (or keep all those chunky bits in for extra deliciousness) and serve!

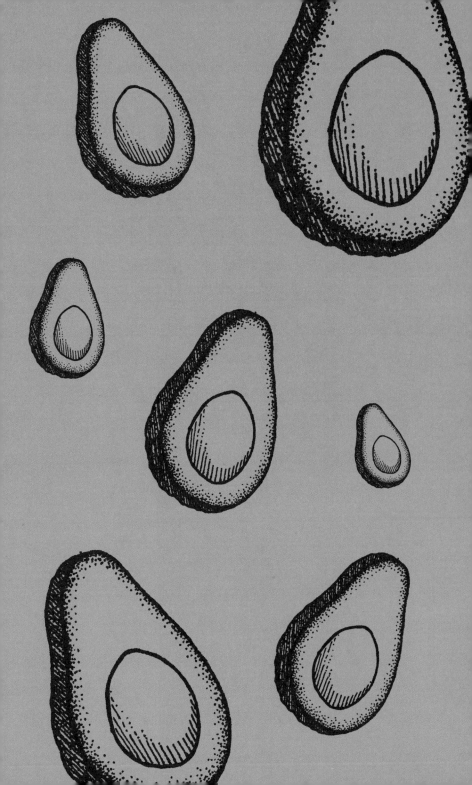

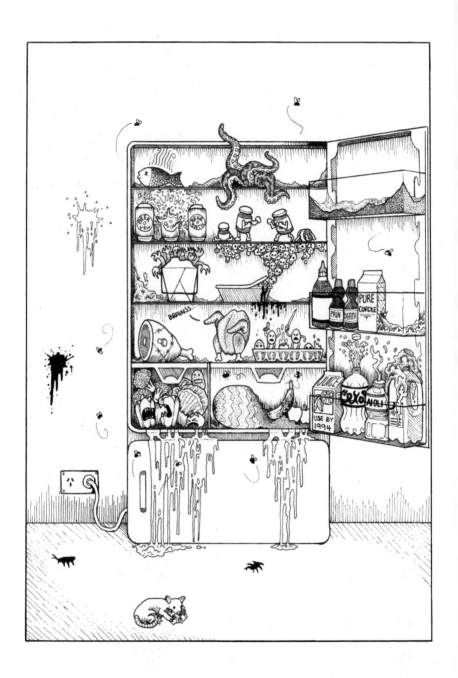

DRINKING OFF MILK: DEATH, DESPAIR AND DISGUST

Surprisingly, use-by dates exist for a reason. When milk is pasteurised, the process kills off most of the nasty bacteria. However, there are organisms called thermoduric bacteria that survive the pasteurisation process in small quantities. These bacteria develop slowly within the milk, even when you keep it in the fridge.

The result of consuming thermoduric bacteria is food poisoning. Unfortunately for us all, the severity of this food poisoning ranges from mild to horrific; the main side effects being cramping, nausea, diarrhoea and fever, which generally last for 48 hours. Fortunately, there are ways to lessen your sad, dairy-induced affliction.

STAY HYDRATED

Fluids are your friends. Get as many electrolytes in your system as you can stomach (which may not be many given your current state). Coconut water, sports drinks, and those little effervescent electrolyte tablets that look like a primary-school volcano when you drop them in water, are all necessities.

TEA

There are very few problems in life that can't be solved with a hot cup of tea. Decaffeinated teas like chamomile, peppermint and dandelion can help soothe your upset stomach.

CARBS

When you're somewhat resembling a normal human again, and able to think about food without wanting to die in a pool of your own vomit, focus on carbs as your reintroduction to the world of eating. Plain crackers, rice, oats (made with water, not milk – stay away from dairy until you're fully recovered), toast, and potatoes.

AVOID

Dairy, duh... Anything spicy is a definite no-go, and same goes for fatty or fried foods.

Sadly, there is no cure for food poisoning – the easiest solution is to check before you consume, and try to be an organised and responsible adult who buys fresh milk every once in a while.

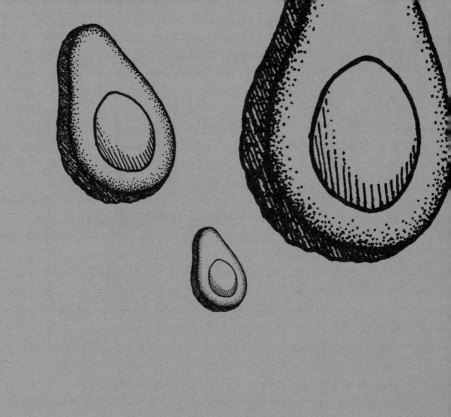

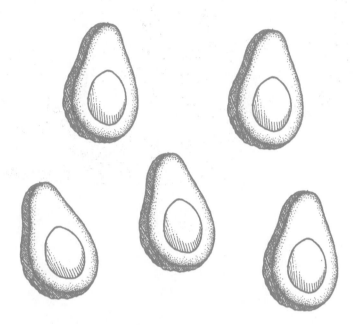

STOCKING UP

Making stock is another essential cooking skill that will fool people into thinking you actually know what you're doing with your life, and probably assist you in not getting scurvy from your steady diet of mi goreng and mac and cheese.

Stock is basically a compilation of the vegetables that have been slowly deteriorating at the bottom of your fridge.

Keep in mind that if all you put in your stock is carrot and salt, you're basically making carrot-water. Err on the side of caution and try to get as much goodness in that pot as possible.

What You'll Need

The following is a general guideline of helpful (but not essential) ingredients:

LEFTOVER BEEF, LAMB OR CHICKEN BONES *(herbivores, feel free to disregard)*

1 ONION

6 CLOVES GARLIC

4 LARGE CARROTS

4 CELERY STALKS

PARSLEY

PEPPERCORNS

3 BAY LEAVES

SALT

OPTIONAL DRIED HERBS *(feel free to add a dash of whatever dried seasoning you can find lurking in the depths of your pantry)*

1   Wash your vegetables thoroughly and roughly chop them into manageable sizes.

2   Chuck veggies, optional meat bones and miscellaneous herbs and spices into a large pot, then add enough water to cover all your ingredients.

3   Put your concoction over a medium–low heat and leave to bubble away for 3–4 hours. Skim any foam off the top as needed, and as the water level drops, continue to add more so veggies remain covered.

4   Strain out all the chunky bits and you're done! This fantastically basic nutritional necessity can keep in your fridge for up to 4 days and can be frozen for 4–6 months.

If you choose to freeze your stock, do it in batches, so when you need to defrost it you'll have manageable portions rather than litres of thawing meat and veggie juice.

Shit you should know

THE STEAKS ARE HIGH

Even the most under-skilled cook has a vague idea of how to switch on a barbecue and produce a cooked steak. However, if you're looking to feast on a piece of meat that isn't a hunk of charcoal by the time you're finished with it, having a general idea of how to create a passable steak is an essential skill.

There are a number of things that can affect the speed and consistency of your steak cooking, including, but not limited to, the temperature before cooking, the cut, and what implements you use to cook your hunk of meat. But there are a few tricks to obtain that perfect level of steak doneness.

The first is temperature. For this, you'll need to equip yourself with a thermometer, and not one of those medical ones your mum used to stick under your tongue when you were faking a sickie.

There are six main types of steak doneness, each of which has an optimal temperature.

- ✳ **Blue**: 55°C
- ✳ **Rare**: 60°C
- ✳ **Medium rare**: 60–65°C
- ✳ **Medium**: 65–70°C
- ✳ **Medium well**: 70°C
- ✳ **Well done**: 75°C

The second handy test for determining the doneness of that choice slab is the hand test. This is conducted via a series of hand gestures (sadly not the lewd kind). By placing a finger to the fleshy part of your hand beneath your thumb, you can get a feel for the ideal consistency of a perfectly cooked steak. Remember: one hand is for gestures, the other is for fondling. Don't try this single-handedly, it will not work out for you.

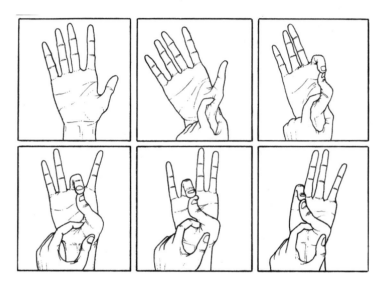

Rare: Relax one hand, then with your other hand, feel the fleshy section of your palm. It should feel quite soft.

Medium rare: Gently place the tips of your thumb and index finger together in an 'ok' gesture and fondle that fleshy part. It will feel springy.

Medium: Resist the urge to give someone the finger, and instead place your middle finger against your thumb.

Medium well: Touch your ring finger to your thumb. The fleshy part should now be firm to the touch.

Well done: Place your pinky against your thumb. For this final level of doneness, the fleshy part should be firm and hard (that's what she said... I'm sorry, it had to be done).

While these tips will help you assess how cooked your steak is, they are not a remedy for terrible culinary practices. So, to avoid destroying your steak:

* **Be consistent** with your cooking times: if you cook one side for two minutes, do the same to the other.
* **If you're cooking on a barbecue**, don't turn it up to full blast and close the lid; this is how to make charcoal, not dinner.
* **Finally, and most importantly**, keep your eyes on the prize. This goes for all things cooking related. Don't turn the heat on and walk away. Again, we're making dinners not insurance claims – I won't be held accountable for your house burning down while you attempt not to be hopeless at life.

Shit you should know

It's important to note that, just like you after getting totally cooked, meat needs a little rest. Keep in mind that meat will continue to cook while resting, so to make sure you don't overcook your steak, always cook 3–6°C below the ideal temperature.

WAYS TO PREPARE AVOCADO (BECAUSE LET'S FACE IT, YOU'RE NEVER GOING TO BUY A HOUSE)

Possibly one of the most important culinary skills for the modern millennial is the art of avocado preparation. It's a well-known fact that in addition to our memes, confusing acronyms and hipster tendencies, our dependency on smashed avo is the main reason all of us will be living with our parents into our late forties. Avocado may just be the cause and solution to all our problems.

GUACAMOLE

Fresh, classic and delicious enough to trick people into believing its preparation might have taken a little skill.

What You'll Need

1 AVOCADO

¼ RED ONION, FINELY CHOPPED

1 BIRD'S EYE CHILLI, THINLY SLICED

¼ CUP CORIANDER, ROUGHLY CHOPPED

½ LEMON OR LIME

SALT AND PEPPER TO SEASON

1   Cut your avo in half, remove the seed and scoop all that green goodness into a bowl. Mash with a fork until avo has a chunky, paste-like consistency.

2   Mix in onion, chilli and coriander.

3   Squeeze lemon (or lime) onto avo mixture, then add a dash of salt and pepper.

4   That's literally it. Consume with chips or shovel out of the bowl with your fingers like the animal you are.

SMASHED AVO FT. TOAST

This is the pinnacle of the millennial dining experience, and all-round bloody good time for your tastebuds. Whether it's part of a twenty-three-dollar breakfast complete with cold-drip coffee with a dash of macadamia milk, or a budget meal, artfully placed on that piece of wholegrain toast that's been frosting over in your freezer for months, you really can't go wrong with smashed avo.

What You'll Need

1 AVOCADO

SALT AND PEPPER

OPTIONAL SEASONINGS:
CHILLI FLAKES, GARLIC,
LEMON, LIME

TOAST

OPTIONAL TOPPINGS:
FETA CHEESE, GOAT'S
CHEESE, POACHED EGG,
SMOKED SALMON, PESTO,
RED ONION, SLIVERED
ALMONDS, PEPITAS, BACON
– probably not all at once, but hey, who am I to judge?

1   Cut avocado in half, remove seed and dump that glorious green goop into a bowl.
2   Season with salt, pepper and anything in your cupboard, really. Avocado goes with everything.
3   Smash.
4   Smear on toast.
5   If you're feeling really bloody fancy, top with crumbled feta and a poached egg and enjoy the most delicious breakfast combination known to man. If it's a choice between avo and the housing market, I know what I'm choosing.

FLAVOURSOME

There are some painfully gifted beings among us who step into a kitchen and miraculously produce divine dishes that take you to new heights of deliciousness. There are others who set tea towels on fire and think charcoal is the perfect topping for toast… This guide is a helpful cheat sheet for the latter. When in doubt, these classic flavour combinations will save you from culinary disaster.

SWEET

Blueberry	Lemon
Apple	Cinnamon
Honey	Almond
Pineapple	Mint
Strawberries	Cream
Chocolate	Hazelnut
Peanut Butter	Chocolate

SAVOURY

Dill	Smoked Salmon
Tomato	Basil
Peas	Mint
Rosemary	Potato
Garlic	Potato
Parsley	Potato
Cheese	Potato
Butter	Potato*
Lime	Chilli
Beef	Mustard
Pork	Apple
Lamb	Rosemary
Lamb	Mint
Duck	Orange
Blue Cheese	Pear
Ham	Cheese

*Full disclosure: Everything goes with potato. It is the perfect
vegetable and one of the best things about being alive.

EGG-BOILING FOR THE INEPT

Boiled eggs come in two delicious and extravagant varieties: hard boiled and soft boiled. Crafting these delicacies all on your lonesome can be accomplished by following a few simple steps.

What You'll Need

1 SMALL SAUCEPAN

WATER

1 EGG

SLOTTED SPOON

TIMER

1   Procure your small saucepan and fill with enough water to cover an egg by about 1 cm.

2   Bring water to the boil and gently lower in your egg using a slotted spoon – if you like to live dangerously, use you hand and get ready for the adrenalin rush that comes from avoiding the splashback. If making multiple eggs, lower them in one at a time.

3   Reduce the water from a boil to a simmer and set a timer. Your desired yolk consistency will determine the boiling time. For a soft, liquidy yolk, boil for 5 minutes, while 7 minutes will give you an egg with a firmer (although still creamy) yolk.

* Use room-temperature eggs. They're less likely to crack and make gooey egg monsters in your saucepan.
* Use a small saucepan. The bigger the pan, the more likely your eggs are to go crazy and bash into each other, again causing spillage of those precious egg juices.
* If the egg is fresh, allow for an extra 30 seconds of boiling time.

Shit you should know

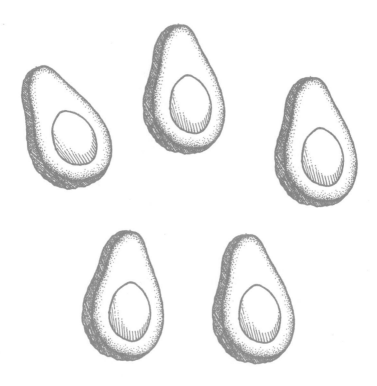

PASTA: THERE IS NO APPROPRIATE SERVING SIZE

It is a truth universally acknowledged that every person who attempts to make a single serving of pasta will end up with enough to feed a small family and inevitably be forced to eat said gargantuan portion of pasta and feel eternal shame at their own inadequate adulting abilities. Fortunately for us, the food gods have deemed that a single serving of pasta is somewhere between 80–100 g. The appropriate way to measure this portion differs from pasta to pasta.

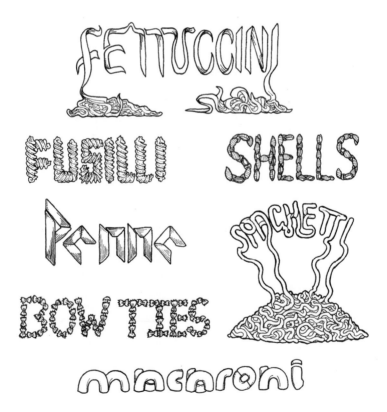

LONG PASTA
(spaghetti, fettuccini, spaghettini, basically any kind of pasta with an "i" on the end):

Let me drop a big knowledge bomb on you. You've probably noticed that most pasta claws have a hole in the centre. This is there to measure out a single serving of pasta. Yep, we've been using the pasta claw wrong our whole lives. If your serving of pasta fits in the hole, you've got enough for one!

If you're on the lower end of the functioning adult spectrum and use a fork in lieu of a pasta claw, there is another slightly less sophisticated way to determine your long-pasta quantities. A regular spaghetti package contains around 400 g, and the recommended serving of pasta is approximately one fifth of this. Bundle your pasta up into five little handfuls, and you'll have the perfect pasta portion, and five hands full of spaghetti…

SHORT PASTA
(elbow macaroni, shell pasta, bow ties):

The serving guideline for short pasta is 57 g, equivalent to ½ cup.

HOLLOW PASTA
(penne):

Like short pasta, the serving guideline is 57 g, but with hollow pasta this is equivalent to ¾ cup.

ICE COLD: HOW LONG CAN THINGS LIVE IN THE FREEZER?

Anyone living out of home knows that frozen goods are the key to financial and dietary success. Storing things in the freezer for too long won't kill you, but it will begin to degrade the quality of your food. If you're game to scrape away the freezer snow and eat a sad, ice-burned snack, then by all means disregard the following recommendations and continue on with your depressing life of unfulfilling frozen meals.

---

* *When defrosting food, never leave it in a warm place – this is how bacteria grows.*
* *When defrosting meat, place on a tray to catch juices. Small pieces of meat should take around 6 hours, whereas large pieces can take up to 48 hours.*

Shit you should know

MEAT

* **Beef**: 12 months
* **Lamb**: 9 months
* **Pork and poultry**: 6 months
* **Cooked or ground meats**: 3 months
* **White fish**: 6–8 months
* **Oily fish (like salmon or mackerel)**: 3–4 months
* **Leftovers containing meat or poultry**: 2–6 months
* **Bacon**: 1 month

FRUIT AND VEGETABLES

* **Blanched vegetables**: 10–12 months
* **Unblanched vegetables**: 3–4 months
* **Vegetable or fruit puree**: 6–8 months
* **Snap-frozen fruit**: 6–8 months

DAIRY

* **Milk**: 3 months
* **Cheese**: 6 months
* **Butter**: 6 months
* **Ice cream**: 2 months

OTHER

* **Breads and cakes**: 3 months
* **Dough**: 3 months

WINE NOT?

As much as it pains me to say, there comes a point in every millennial's life where it's no longer appropriate to be drinking from a goon sack. And when that time comes, it's important to be able to at least pretend you understand the subtle flavour characteristics and food pairings of a drink that is essentially the adult version of a juice box.

Being able to detect tannins, describe robust flavours and use fancy floral words to describe your wine are truly the high points of adult existence. Here's a quick guide to the wine world to help you curate the wine-wanker image you so desperately want.

THE DIFFERENCE BETWEEN RED AND WHITE

Mate, one is red, one is white. If that much wasn't clear to you, you're going to need a whole lot more help than can be found within these pages…

* **Types of grape:** Red and white wines are made with different grape varieties. The colour of the wine itself comes from the skin of the grapes, and the depth of colour is dependent on how long the skin is left in the fermentation process.
* **Tannins:** These are a bitter, naturally occurring substance that give you that dry and puckered mouthfeel – something that sounds a lot dirtier than it is – while drinking. Tannins are caused by the fermentation of the grape skin as the wine matures. Red wines contain more tannins than white.

WHITES

SAUVIGNON BLANC
aka Sav Blanc, aka the wine that is impossible to abbreviate without sounding like a bogan

Sav Blanc has a herbal character, and its flavour is often compared to sour green fruits like apples, pears and melons, as well as white peach or passionfruit – it's pretty much a fruit salad in a glass. Its bright aroma and acidic finish make it the perfect summer wine. Sav Blanc pairs well with fresh, tangy herbs like parsley, basil, coriander and mint, as well as briny, sour flavours like goat's cheese and crème fraîche.

RIESLING

If you're just coming off the goon sack and still prone to ordering the 'house white' at your local, Riesling is probably not the drink for you. German Rieslings have an intense and complex aroma, with flavours of orchard fruits like nectarines, apricots, apples and pears, with a hint of jasmine and a dash of petrol or kerosene (yep, this is an actual thing and it's because of a chemical compound called TDN, which is a product of the ripeness or age of the wine). Petrol-taste aside, Riesling is the perfect match for spicy foods and rich proteins. Australian Rieslings have high acidity and a citrusy aroma, and pair well with seafood.

PINOT GRIS OR PINOT GRIGIO
(they're basically the same thing and only super-fancy wine-wankers are going to pull you up on the differentiation)

This wine has a citrus flavour and zesty aroma, with notes of lime, lemon and pear. This pinot can sometimes have a honey flavour depending on where the grapes are grown. Perfect for your light, boozy lunch of fresh veggies and flaky white fish. Try to avoid anything too spicy with this one!

CHARDONNAY

The most popular of the white wines, served still or sparkling. Chardonnay has a voluptuous taste, often described as buttery, and is best served with soft cheeses, rich sauces (an obvious accompaniment to your béchamel!) and fatty fishes like salmon.

SEMILLON

Full-bodied and strong. Describing the taste of a Semillon is like describing the physique of a female body-builder. Semillon has a fig-like taste and is often mixed with Sav Blanc to balance out the strong flavours. This wine goes well with bold, aromatic dishes and woody spices like cinnamon and star anise. It's often referred to as the perfect sushi wine, as it also goes with raw fish and ginger.

MOSCATO

Here's a fun fact to impress all your new wine-wanker friends: Moscato is made from one of the oldest wine grapes in the world! This wine has a sweet and fruity taste reminiscent of peaches and orange blossom. Its flavours complement spicy foods and fragrant spices like ginger, cinnamon and cardamom, making it the best pairing for Thai or Vietnamese food. Serve chilled.

REDS

PINOT NOIR

This is one of the lighter-coloured reds, made from little bitch-ass grapes that are prone to disease and mutations, but delicious nonetheless. Despite the sad little grapes that produce it, Pinot Noir is actually a great match for lots of food because it's both light and complex. With its fruity notes of cranberry, cherry and raspberry, this all-rounder is the prime choice for those moments when you want to be a grown-up, but still can't quite figure out which wine is which.

MERLOT

This dark, voluptuous wine is filled with flavours of plum and black cherry, and often has a vanilla aroma. Its smooth finish is not the only reason why this wine should become your new go-to; Merlots are renowned for being on the cheaper end of the spectrum – just like you after a few glasses! Merlot pairs well with most foods, but is particularly good with chicken and lightly spiced dark meats.

SHIRAZ

Great news: Shiraz is filled with a whole bunch of antioxidants, which basically makes it a grown-up green juice, so the health benefits of this wine will allow you to justify your terrible drinking habits. Shiraz, also known as Syrah, has fruity, berry flavours like blackberry, blueberry and boysenberry, and a smoky aroma. Shiraz pairs perfectly with bold foods, like blue cheese, barbecued meats or floral herbs like fennel.

CABERNET SAUVIGNON

Cab Sav is a full-bodied big red, and comes with dark fruit flavours and a hint of black pepper. This is the ultimate wine-wanker drink – a glass must always be in hand while discussing notes of this and hints of that. Extra points if you use the word aroma. The perfect drink for rich, meaty dishes. Once you've mastered your steak, this is the wine you want.

AN OVERVIEW OF THE FANCY WINE TERMS YOU CAN USE TO DESCRIBE THAT TEN-DOLLAR BOTTLE YOU GRABBED FROM ALDI:

* **Grippy tannins:** You know when your mouth feels all puckered and dry after you've gulped down that glass of house red? This is because of those pesky tannins, and rather than grandly announcing, 'That drop gave me wicked dry-mouth' why not class it up a little with, 'I do say, the grippy tannins in that Shiraz are extraordinarily dry on the palate.'

* **Austere:** This is one you'll be using fairly often. Austere describes wines that are overly acidic and usually pretty trash.

* **Body:** Picture this – you're sitting with your rich friends by the fire, holding a comically large glass of Merlot, and looking for the perfect word to describe that delightful drop and prove yourself the fancy wine-wanker you know you are. The word 'full-bodied' slips from your lips, and just like that, everyone knows you're a true wine connoisseur. Full-bodied, medium-bodied and light-bodied are the perfect words to express the weight or feel of wine in your mouth. Generally, the weightier or more full-bodied a wine is, the higher the alcohol content. Score.

✳ **Finish:** This is basically just a fancy word for 'aftertaste'. The type of finish varies from wine to wine, but some useful (and not at all pretentious) finishing buzzwords are smoky, sweet, harsh, spicy, rigid and citrusy. Use them wisely.

✳ **Sommelier, aka wine genius:** Sommeliers are experts in all things wine. Although it's fairly safe to assume you're not fancy enough to even set foot in a place that has one, knowing what these wine service gods are called might make you sound like you occasionally drink somewhere other than the local RSL.

✳ **Decanter:** Getting into real fancy wine accoutrement here, a decanter is a device used to introduce oxygen to your wine, a process which smooths out tannins and is said to create a better drinking experience. I'm somewhat unsure about the demographic of people who actually have time to wait to drink their wine once the bottle has been opened, but maybe knowing what a decanter is will allow you to curate the image of yourself as a person who drinks for pleasure, visits wine country (every wine-wanker knows the Hunter Valley is so overrated!) and sails around on a yacht, laughing about negative gearing.

COFFEE: FROM EUPHORIA TO ANXIETY ATTACKS

Coffee: the bean of the gods, liquid of the heavens and my number-one reason to keep living. I think we can all agree that coffee is one of the best things about being an adult human. That being said, there's no greater terror than the anxiety of choosing the perfect form for your life-force to take.

LONG BLACK

This is the coffee for no-nonsense people who literally DGAF. Big ol' cups of black coffee served with no sugar or milk so as to not alter the flavour. The ultimate drink for your favourite coffee addict.

ICED COFFEE

Reason #100,000,000 why coffee is the third-most popular drink in the world (after water and tea, which are realistically just less exciting versions of coffee anyway): it's delicious in all climates. A shot of coffee mixed with ice and enough ice cream to make an imminent caffeine heart attack a sugary certainty, these delicious and refreshing drinks are not to be confused with the iced latte, an ice-cream-less alternative to the traditional cold-coffee treat.

ESPRESSO

Also known as a short black, this is the concentrated hit of coffee you probably don't need but are going to have anyway because you're an adult and can make your own decisions. These tiny shots of gunpowder are made by forcing boiling water through very finely ground beans. Like long blacks, no milk or extras are added.

AMERICANO

The long blacks for those who just aren't hardcore enough. An Americano is a watered-down long black, made popular by American soldiers who were attempting to ration their coffee – the perfect drink for nerds who care if they're hydrated or not.

LATTE

The coffee to order when you're just dipping your toe into that black pool of anxiety-ridden deliciousness. Lattes are made with foamed milk, a much-appreciated addition that masks the bitter taste of the coffee.

FLAT WHITE

Basically the same as a latte (don't tell the coffee-wankers I said that), just less foamy and made with bottom-of-the-barrel milk that, in addition to being icky, gives the coffee a smoother consistency.

CAPPUCCINO

One of the most horrific things about transitioning into the adult world is that it's no longer socially acceptable to order a babyccino when you go out for breakfast. Thankfully, there's a solution. The cappuccino is a shot of espresso, mixed with a delightfully fluffy layer of foamy milk. Drinking a cappuccino is the equivalent of drinking an anxious cloud and I am all about that life.

MACCHIATO

If you want your espresso with a little extra sparkle, a macchiato is the way to go. A shot of espresso topped with a dash of foamy milk – it's all about that garnish.

MOCHA

Coffee for beginners. An espresso combined with hot milk and chocolate, a mocha is basically a grown-up hot chocolate.

PICCOLO LATTE

Lattes for people with tiny bladders: the middle ground between a latte an espresso. Perfect for people who can only handle minimal coffee-breath.

VIENNA

Caffeine and sugar addicts rejoice in this mind-bending combination. A double-espresso shot with whipped cream in lieu of milk, a Vienna is sometimes even topped with chocolate sprinkles, just in case it wasn't sweet enough.

AFFOGATO

Only the best dessert in the entire world, an affogato is one delightful and creamy scoop of vanilla ice cream topped with a hot shot of espresso. Be an adult and a kid all at once.

IRISH COFFEE

If I had to pick one beverage to drink for the rest of my life, this would be it. Hot coffee, Irish whiskey, sugar and thick cream. Sweet, delicious and boozy, it's the trifecta of perfection.

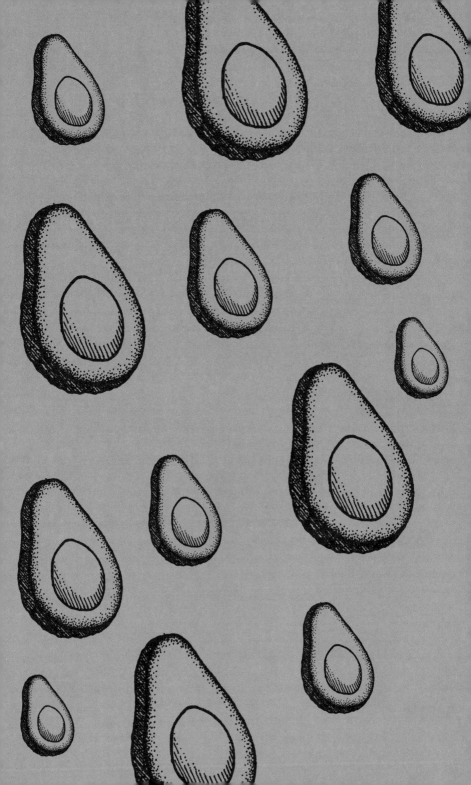

COOKING = SCIENCE: ARE BICARB AND BAKING POWDER THE SAME THING?

It's a question everyone has asked themselves a thousand times, and the answer is, 'No, stupid.'

Why can't things be simple?

* Bicarbonate of soda and baking soda are the same thing. In Australia and the UK, it's referred to as bicarbonate of soda or bicarb soda, whereas in America, it's referred to as baking soda.
* Both bicarb soda and baking powder are used as leavening agents. A leavening agent is a substance that reacts to acidic compounds, causing a release of carbon dioxide to form little air pockets in batter, making it lighter and fluffier.

Bicarb soda is a slightly salty chemical compound ($NaHCO_3$) comprised of sodium bicarbonate.

There are several acidic elements that help induce the chemical reaction in bicarb soda, including cream of tartar, lemon juice, yoghurt, buttermilk, cocoa and vinegar. Bicarb is generally found in pancakes, cakes, soda bread and baked goods with a light, spongy consistency.

Bicarb soda is about 3–4 times stronger than baking powder. Cooking is an art, but baking is a science, so if you don't follow the recipe and measure your portions, you're going to end up with a deflated bar of soap instead of delicious brownies.

Baking powder is a mix of acid (in the form of cream of tartar) an alkali (aka bicarb soda) and a tiny bit of inert stabiliser (usually cornstarch). While baking powder contains bicarb soda, the extra ingredients mean it requires a liquid stimulant to set off its chemical reaction.

The main purpose of baking powder is to increase the volume and lighten the texture of baked goods. As with bicarb soda, baking powder releases carbon dioxide and has become a staple in most quick bread recipes, such as muffins, banana breads, pizza crusts and scones.

In short, while both ingredients are used as leavening agents and are likely to be found in most baked goods, bicarb soda is a straight chemical compound and reacts with acidic elements, whereas baking powder contains both an acid and an alkali and requires liquid to react. #science

OILY AF: DISPOSING OF OIL

Fun fact: oil and grease cannot be poured down the drain. Fat solidifies, and although pouring it down the drain creates a nice 'out of sight, out of mind' experience, once that oil is gone, it begins to build up in the pipes, eventually leading to sewerage overflows. To avoid these disgusting and potentially expensive issues and general pipe-related ickiness, here are the best ways to dispose of kitchen oils and greases.

* For oils that solidify, like animal fats, butter or shortening, place them in a sealable (and disposable) container and leave in the fridge.* Once the oil has solidified, throw the entire container away with your regular garbage.
  *Given the crisis-state of our planet, using a non-biodegradable or plastic container is not advisable.
* If you're unable to find a biodegradable container, put your oil in a bowl in the fridge, allow the oil to harden, then scoop it out into a compostable bag and place this in your normal trash. Wait as close to garbage day as possible to avoid any leakage in your bin.
* To dispose of used cooking oil, let it cool completely then pour into a container with a lid (wax-lined milk cartons or other sealable wax-lined products are ideal) and include it in your normal garbage.
* If you don't have a disposable container, you can mix oil with something absorbent, like sand, flour or sawdust.
* Cooking oils, such as olive or canola, can be reused; perfect for those moments when you're just too poor for such extravagances. After deep-frying, used cooking oil can be strained through a coffee filter to remove any waste. The oil can then be stored in an airtight container before it's used again. Make

sure to smell the oil before cooking – it can be used up to two times after your first fry-up, but if it smells rancid, it's time for an oil change!

✳ Some local waste departments will accept cooking oils, so before you dispose of them, check with your local council. To dispose of oil at the tip, use the biodegradable container strategy!

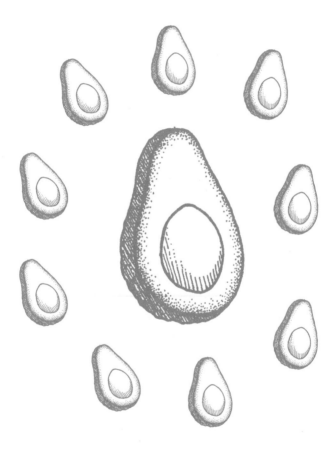

IS YOUR OVEN AS FILTHY AS YOU?

Does everything you bake taste like charcoal? Is there an unexplained plume of black smoke that rises from your oven every time you turn it on? If so, that bad boy is likely dirtier than you are, and needs a good scrubbing.

If you're looking for an oven-cleaning solution that's both cheap, environmentally friendly and easy, you've come to the right place.

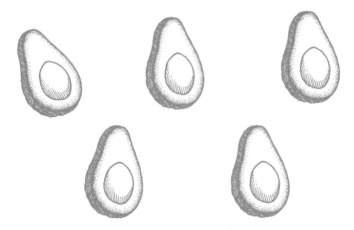

What You'll Need

½ CUP BAKING SODA

2–3 TABLESPOONS WATER

1 OLD CLEANING CLOTH

½ CUP VINEGAR

1 SPRAY BOTTLE

1. Combine baking soda and water to form a paste.

2. Spread the paste inside your oven, covering everything but the heating element, and allow to sit for 12 hours.

3. After the paste has sunk into that oven grime, take a damp cloth (preferably one you're not overly attached to) and wipe out as much of the paste as you can.

4. Add vinegar to a spray bottle and spritz away – you should see a fizzy reaction between the vinegar and any residual baking soda.

5. Wipe out all the vinegar and remaining baking soda. You may need to do this a couple of times.

6. There you have it. A clean oven, with no crazy chemicals. Just like a real grown-up!

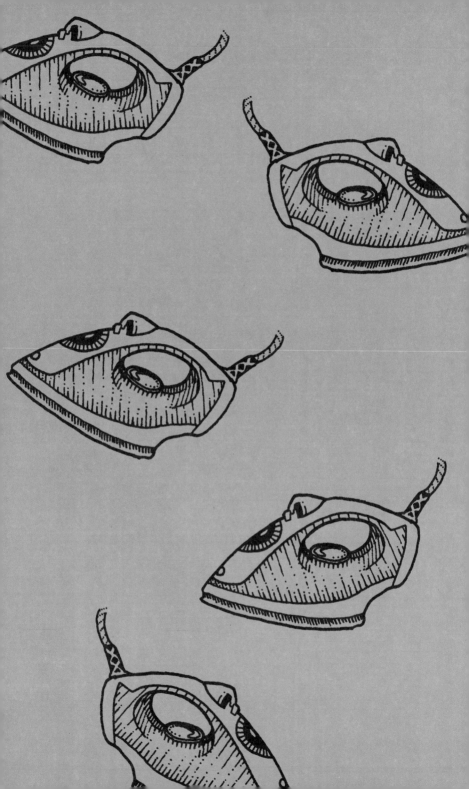

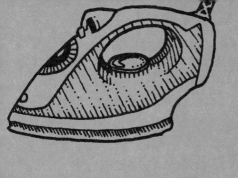
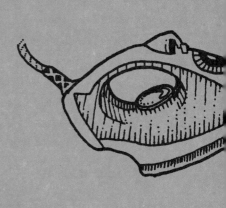

LIVING
OUT OF
HOME

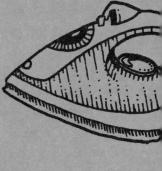

WITHOUT DYING

WHEN I WAS A KID, all I wanted was to move out of home. To me, having my own place was the ultimate sign of adulthood, and I couldn't wait to reach that peak level of maturity.

I planned to stay up all night, eat chocolate cake for breakfast, and watch whatever trashy TV I wanted without judgement or complaints. Well, it turns out that now I actually do live out of home, I'm in bed by 9.30 and only eat chocolate cake for breakfast when I'm having a mental breakdown. On the bright side, I watch as much of *The Simpsons* as I want, and my encyclopedic knowledge of quotes has proven to be a beneficial life skill.

I have also had to learn a harsh reality of adult life: living out of home means you have to keep yourself alive. For someone who struggles to keep a plant green for more than 24 hours, this is a somewhat daunting task. The following is an informative exploration into the things you need to know to help you cling to life, and keep you from begging your parents to take you back and wishing you'd never progressed past eight years of age.

I DON'T GIVE A SHEET: HOW TO MAKE YOUR BED

What You'll Need

The self-explanatory:

A BED

A MATTRESS

The materials:

MATTRESS PROTECTOR

FITTED SHEET

SINGLE SHEET (optional)

DOONA AND COVER

PILLOWS
(number dependent on comfort and/or level of loneliness)

PILLOWCASES

Mattress protectors are actually super important additions to your sleeping set-up. Not only do they protect you from allergens such as bed bugs and dust mites, but they also protect the mattress itself from water damage and stains. The average person loses around 200 ml of sweat per 8 hours of sleep. The human body is gross, but your mattress doesn't have to be.

Shit you should know

1   **Put on the mattress protector**
    Figure out which way the protector goes on to avoid
    the awkward dance of putting it on, taking it off, and
    then doing the whole thing three more times until you
    eventually figure it out. Pro tip: The tag always goes on
    the bottom right-hand corner. You're welcome.

    ✳   Tuck the elastic edges of the protector around
        the mattress.
    ✳   Smooth down to remove any creases or lumps.

2   **Add the fitted sheet**
    A fitted sheet is essentially a less bulky version of the
    mattress protector. Follow the same steps as above;
    I'm not writing them out for you again, you lazy shit.

3   **Top sheet**
    To me, top sheets seem like a complete waste of space,
    and their addition to any bed should be completely
    optional. However, like so many seemingly unnecessary
    aspects of adulthood, top sheets are one of those items
    that scream 'I'm an adult'. If you haven't noticed how very
    little faith I have in your ability to adult, let me explain this
    extraordinarily simple task to you in explicit detail.

    ✳   Find the largest hem of the sheet. This goes at the
        top of the bed.
    ✳   Align the hem with the head of the bed, and
        smooth the sheet over the bed, tucking the
        corners under the mattress.
    ✳   We could go into the dreaded hospital corner
        here, but to be honest, they're pointless, useless
        and a waste of everyone's time.

4   **Doona cover**
 ✳   Turn the doona cover inside out.
 ✳   Act like a ghost and get right up inside the cover
     by putting your arms all the way through until you
     can grab the corners.
 ✳   Pick up the two corners of the smallest edge of
     the doona with your cover-clad hands.
 ✳   Now for the tricky part: flip the cover the correct
     way while still holding the doona inside.
 ✳   Pull the cover down to fully encase the doona.
 ✳   Do up the buttons/zipper/velcro that seals the
     end of the cover.
 ✳   Place doona across the bed.

5   **Pillows and cases**
 ✳   A literal child could do this without instruction.
     Slip the pillows into their respective cases, making
     sure to close up the seam or fold on the end.
 ✳   Place pillows artfully on the bed, possibly
     adding an array of impractical extras to make
     you look fancy.

*Making a bed is substantially easier with a partner, and this
should be the main incentive for venturing into a romantic
relationship. If you are without a partner, you might as well
just invest in a sleeping bag and get cosy on the floor, you
poor, lonely soul.*

Shit you should know

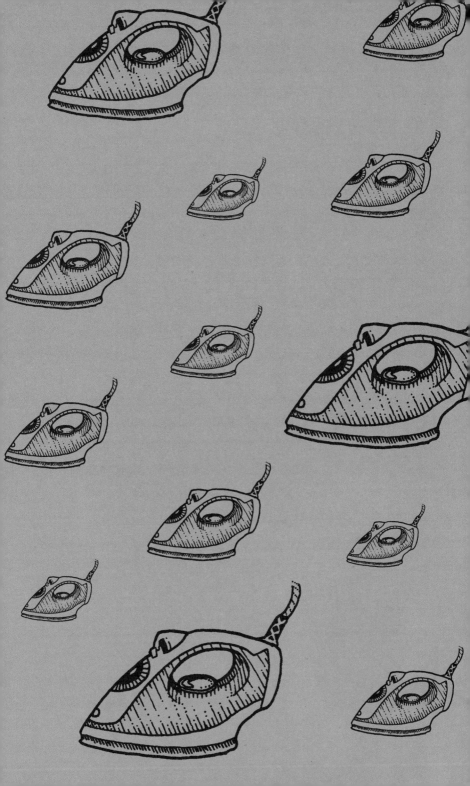

ARE YOU LIVING IN YOUR OWN FILTH?

The quickest way to ditch your trash-human vibe is to look at the etiquette for when you should wash and replace basic household items… It turns out that bedsheets are meant to be washed at least once a week. At the time of writing, I couldn't remember the last time I'd washed my sheets. I am filthy and disgusting and probably the reason Jesus cries at night.

After discovering that bedsheets are meant to be changed far more often than is humanly possible, I also stumbled across the unsettling knowledge that there are many, many things within our houses that need to be washed or disposed of completely on a regular basis. Read this list and tremble in terror at your own inadequate adulting skills and generally unsanitary habits.

> *Did you know that things used to clean other things need to be cleaned too? I sure as hell didn't. Turns out both your washing machine AND dishwasher need to be cleaned regularly. For years, my white clothes have been coming out of the wash with weird and unexplained stains; I finally understand that this was my washing machine crying out for help. Washing machines should be sprayed and cleaned twice a month to prevent bacteria, mould and limescale. Dishwashers should be put through a hot wash with a cup of white vinegar once a month to kill off any lingering bacteria and icky smells.*
>
> Shit you should know

WHEN TO CLEAN

Kitchen sponges	*Rinse every day, throw away every week.*
Towels	*Wash after 3 uses (USES, PEOPLE, NOT DAYS!)*
Tea towels	*Wash EVERY. DAMN. DAY.*
Pillows	*Wash every 3 months – if your head is anywhere near as dirty as your mind, you may need to consider doing this more frequently.*
Phones	*Every. Single. Day.*
Bras	*The eternal struggle of every woman, or hefty-chested man: every 2–3 days.*
Light switches (cue the I-don't-think-I've-ever-washed-a-light-switch-in-my-life terror)	*Once a week.*
Remote controls	*Once a month.*
Fridge	*Disinfect and wipe out every week.*

WHEN TO DISPOSE OF*	
Tupperware	*Every 3 months.*
Chopping board	*Every year.*
Mattress	*Every 8 years.*
Toothbrush	*Every month.*

*The sad and sorry state of the environment is just one of the horrible things we get to fret about in our adulthood. While disposing of plastics regularly is sanitary, it isn't a sustainable practice – environmentally or financially. Invest in glass food storage, bamboo toothbrushes and wooden chopping boards to lessen your impact on the planet and your wallet.

I may be a hopeless adult, but I'm also a realist. Ain't nobody got time for all that cleaning. Keep living in your trash heap, I won't judge you. Just sit with the knowledge that you are bad, and you should feel bad, and that there are some people out there who actually clean out their entire fridge every bloody week…

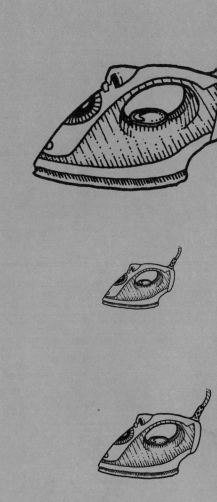

FOLDING FITTED SHEETS: MAKE THE MYTH A REALITY

I once believed that folding a fitted sheet was an adulting urban legend; a skill only to be dreamed of, but never actually accomplished. I convinced myself I didn't really need to know how to fold a fitted sheet anyway; what's wrong with a good old balled-up sheet shoved deep into the back of your cupboard where no one can see your shame? Oh, how wrong I was… I sheet you not, of all my new adulting knowledge, the ability to fold a fitted sheet is one of my most treasured skills. There is no experience that has given me as much pride and satisfaction as making a perfect square out of that unruly tangle of cloth and elastic. Adulty AF.

1   **Lay your sheet out** on a flat surface, grab the bottom corners and turn them inside out. Tuck these into the top corners, aligning the seams to create a rectangle.

2   **Fold your rectangle in half**, with the elastic edges tucked inside themselves.

3   **Fold in half again** so you have a square sheet, and smooth down to remove wrinkles.

4   **Fold sheet into thirds.** Done. In four easy steps you've become an adult.

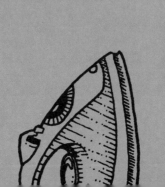

HOW NOT TO BE A PLANT MURDERER

I am a firm believer that keeping a house plant alive is as difficult as keeping a human child alive, if not more so. Those leafy little bastards live to disappoint you, they want you to feel inadequate and underprepared, and they are the physical embodiment of all your failed forays into the adult world.

But no more! I refuse to let my self-worth be determined by the shrivelled corpses of cactuses, or the wilted leaves of a peace lily. Absorb this wisdom for plant happiness and show those photosynthesising tyrants who's boss!

KNOW YOUR PLANT

I understand the very real temptation to buy the coolest-looking plant in the store, but chances are that 200-year-old bonsai you have your eye on is going to require a lot more attention than you are capable of providing. When picking your plant, check the care label; if sun, water and unconditional love are things you're unable to give, maybe invest in a rock instead.

HEY, GOOD LOOKIN'

You can tell a lot about the health of your plant from how they're looking; they don't just exist to be pretty and brighten your life, you selfish arsehole…

* **Dry soil:** This means your plant is dry; shocker, I know. Hydrate until water comes from the drainage holes, because that bitch is thirsty AF.
* **Soaking wet:** You watered your plant a few days ago, and it's still soaking wet. Another shocking revelation on the plant-hydration front, but this means you've

overwatered that bad boy. Check to see if your pot has drainage holes – if not, transfer it to one that does, or make some holes yourself, and then take it easy on the watering until the soil dries.

✳ **New growth:** Is your plant growing new things? No? This probably means that, like you, your plant is stunted and underdeveloped. A light fertiliser may be the answer (keep in mind that for plants, fertiliser does not equal food, so use sparingly).

Plants require three types of nutrients to thrive: nitrogen, phosphorous and potash. These three elements make up the base of most fertilisers.

> ✳ *Nitrogen encourages healthy, green foliage growth.*
> ✳ *Phosphorous encourages root growth.*
> ✳ *Potash encourages bigger, healthier blooms.*

Shit you should know

So, your plant is growing new things, but those things are weak, sad and bringing shame on your plant. It's pretty likely that this sad, ugly plant is begging you for some sunlight. Although fertiliser doesn't equal plant food, sunlight does, so give that thing some sweet sunshine!

LOCATION, LOCATION, LOCATION

Plants are all about that prime real estate.

✳ **Keep away** from extremes; nothing too hot, cold or draughty.
✳ **Move away** from air conditioners or heating vents.
✳ **If your plant's roots are poking out** of the soil, transfer it to a bigger pot with more room to grow.

BROWN SPOTS

Brown spotty leaves on your plant can mean a few things:

* **You're a plant killer:** I mean, we already knew that, but your plant's cries for help will make a bit more sense with a reason behind them. Brown spots on your leaves can mean you're overwatering your plant and drowning the roots.
* **Underwatering:** It seems cruel and confusing that brown spots could mean both over and underwatering, but plants are fickle and want to keep you on your toes.
* **Low humidity:** Like hair, leaves can become dry in low humidity. Give your plant a light spritz 2–3 times a week to help spruce them up and add some volume.

TENDER LOVE 'N' CARE

Just like people, plants need some sweet lovin' from time to time. Keep your plant happy by:

* **Cleaning the dust** off the leaves.
* **Checking for bugs and mites** – if you do find any of these on your precious leaf-baby, give it a quick wash in the shower (it goes without saying, but I'm going to say it anyway because I have no faith in you: don't turn the shower up full blast – a gentle spray is all you need).
* **Removing any dead** or dying leaves so that new growths can flourish.
* **Chatting to it** every now and then. Tell it you love its sweet little leaves and that your plant's presence in your home has saved you from the deep, crushing loneliness of adult life.

Turns out, if you pay attention to your plant, it's not too hard to figure out what it is they need. Just think of all your future house plants as needy babies, covered in lettuce.

WASH YOUR CLOTHES WITHOUT RUINING THEM

Being an adult ruins so many things: the ability to drink without feeling like you're going to die the next day; the use of inexperience as an excuse for stupidity; and most of all, the enjoyment of being a filthy mess without judgement. Let's face it: even people who aren't trash humans still spill shit all over themselves from time to time, and it's an unspoken rule of the universe that all white shirts are destined to be ruined before their time. To my mind, one of the most precious abilities of those whimsical adults who are just too grown-up for their own good is the capacity to throw even the most stained garment in the wash and have it reappear looking fresher than ever. Us mere mortals can only dream of having such abilities, but these tips will help you get a little closer to that godly level of skill.

* **Delicate bags:** These mesh bags cost about $2 and are endlessly useful. Stuff them with your bras, stockings and those undies you save for *special occasions* to avoid destroying all these pretty things that cost so very much.
* **Wash your clothes inside out:** This sounds stupid, but it means any wear and tear that occurs in the wash cycle will only happen to the inside of your garments, so just like you, your clothes will be able to maintain a clean facade that ensures no one will know how ruined they are on the inside.
* **Use the gentle cycle** on your washing machine... even if you don't think you need to. Realistically, what are you washing that needs to be spun around at 100 km/h? You're dirty, but you're not that dirty.
* **Read the care labels:** Although mainly considered

annoyingly itchy addendums to your favourite shirt, these tags actually contain useful information when it comes to preserving your clothes. Deciphering the symbols on these labels is honestly more complicated than reading hieroglyphs. Luckily, there are only nine symbols worth remembering, and if you carry this book around forever, you'll always have the answers to the boring adult questions you never knew you needed the answers to.

Machine wash, do not machine wash and handwash

Do not bleach

Tumble-dry and do not tumble-dry

Do not iron

Dry-clean and do not dry-clean

✳ **Detergent:** This shit should never be put directly on, or left to sit on, your clothes before washing, particularly powdered detergent, which is often harsher on clothes than liquid. It's also important to read the labels before committing to a detergent, and choose the one that best suits your usage, machine and fabric type. There IS a difference between front-loader and top-loader washing detergents.

Top loader vs front loader

Top loaders use more water than front loaders and, as a result, have longer cycles. To compensate for the higher volume of water used in these cycles, detergents developed for top loaders produce more suds, or lather, which is easily washed away by all the extra water. Using this type of detergent in a front loader will generally leave your clothes with a detergent residue, making them look dingy.

Front loaders, on the other hand, use less water and have shorter cycles. These washers work best with High Efficiency (HE) low-sudsing detergent. HE detergents produce less lather and remove all the dirt and soap residue with less water.

Using the wrong detergent will not only make your clothes look sub-par, but it can also damage your washing machine! Isn't being an adult interesting?!

Shit you should know

* **Cold-water wash:** Washing your clothes on a cold cycle is not only a much cheaper alternative to hot water, but cotton, wool, linen and other natural fibres are all known to shrink in warm water. Jeans (particularly dark denim) should also be washed in cold water to avoid colour streaking.

* **Air-drying:** Like warm water, the dryer is expensive and generally works against you when it comes to maintaining the integrity of your clothes. Don't trust the machines; take a break from Goon of Fortune and hang your washing out on the line.

* **Buttons and zippers:** A wash cycle is like a rave: it's squishy, fast paced and there's a concerning amount of unidentifiable fluids everywhere. All your clothes are banging together, disorientated and confused, so undoing the buttons means they're less likely to pull and tear in the chaos (aka rave-cave). The opposite goes for zippers – make sure these are zipped up before washing to avoid them tearing and catching on other clothes.

✳ **Segregation:** Turns out your clothes are prejudiced against more than just colour. While everyone except for you knows that garments should be separated by corresponding colour, washing your clothes by fabric type is another way to prevent damage.

✳ **Stripes:** One of the deepest mysteries of the universe is how to correctly wash striped clothes, particularly black and white stripes. They seem like a contradiction to the fundamental science of clothes washing. Colours and whites together as one? It defies logic. But there are a few ways to make this mind-boggling paradox a little simpler:
   - Always wash on a cold cycle – this helps keep the stripes from fading.
   - Give your stripes an extra rinse cycle to remove excess water and keep the white nice and fresh.
   - If you stain the white of your stripe, use laundry spray NOT bleach. For a more natural alternative, you can use distilled white vinegar (which is also good for cleaning the washing machine itself!) or baking soda.
   - Wash your stripes with other striped colours or whites. Avoid washing them with dark jeans, sweaters or anything red.

✳ **Stains:** There's nothing that ruins your carefully curated adult image more than slopping coffee down your white shirt or having to throw out your favourite dress because there was just no chance you could get that wine stain out… Not that anything like that has ever happened to me. I'm an amazing adult and pretty much perfect in every way. Here are a few tips to removing the most common signs of your sad life failures.

Oil stains, e.g. salad dressing or from spitting frying pans	*Sprinkle with salt and let sit before washing.*
Protein stains, e.g. vomit, sweat and blood	*Alkaline stain removers, like ammonia. Pro tip: Hot water makes protein set, so always use cold water for these.*
Combination stains, e.g. sauces and make-up	*Rinse with cold water, then gently rub detergent on the stain.*
Grass stains	*Soak in cool water with detergent for a minimum of 30 minutes, then wash.*
Mud stains	*Let the mud dry then brush it off. Soak in warm water with 1 teaspoon dish detergent and 1 tablespoon white vinegar. Rinse with cold water.*
Coffee	*For fresh stains, rinse immediately with cold water. Rub with water and detergent, then soak for 30 minutes.*
Alcohol	*Sponge the stain with a small amount of water mixed with detergent or white vinegar.*

OH, THE IRONY

Turns out, ironing isn't rocket science. Here's how to get started on your quest to become a presentable grown-up.

* **Own an iron.**
* **An ironing board helps**, too.
* **If you've been paying attention** at all, you'll have realised that adults actually read the care labels on their clothes, rather than cutting them off because they're itchy and stupid. In addition to telling you whether your clothes can be ironed, the label will also let you know what temperature to do it at, because it's obvious you're totally hopeless and require excessive detail and instruction for everything you do.
* **Iron your clothes inside out**; this way, if you do burn them, no one will ever be able to see your failure. This is especially important for dark colours and fabrics like silk, rayon, linen, velvet, corduroy and textured fabrics.
* **Ironing clothes that are slightly damp** presses out the wrinkles faster and leaves the clothes nice and crisp.
* **When ironing sections** of double thickness (like collars, cuffs, pockets or hems), iron first on the inside, then on the outside to smooth out any final wrinkles.
* **Iron from top to bottom**, along the line of your clothes

to prevent pulling on the seams and stretching your shit out. Don't waste that tedious ironing effort and make sure you hang everything immediately after you finish to maintain the fresh-pressed look.

✳ **When ironing a shirt or dress**, always start from the collar and work your way down.

✳ **To iron pants**, start at the waist. Lie them flat on their side with both legs pressed together in a pant sandwich, then iron down towards the bottom.

FOR THE LAZY

Did you know that ironing is a stupid waste of time? Luckily for the lazy slobs among us – myself included – there is an easier (and far less effective) way!

The instructions are simple, assuming that you are a person who showers occasionally. You may think I have little faith in you, but let's face it: you're reading this book so I really can't make any assumptions... Next time you're about to hop in the shower, grab your wrinkly clothes and hang them in the bathroom. Get it nice and hot in there, and you've got yourself a homemade steamer!

After washing your clothes, you can also hang them out on a coathanger and make gravity do the ironing for you (gravity's ironing skills are passable at best, but in all honesty they're probably better than yours).

SEW YOUR LIFE TOGETHER

Like so many other things in life, sewing is a skill that a hopeless adult like you will likely never master. That being said, there are two relatively easy sewing skills that are definitely worth knowing!

SEWING A BUTTON

1   **Thread your needle** with an equal amount of thread coming from each end. Tie these ends together with a small knot.

2   **Line the button up** with the buttonhole on the other side. Nobody likes a crooked hole.

3   **Starting on the reverse side**, push the needle through the fabric and the hole on the underside of the button, pulling the stitch up and through.

4   **Repeat this motion** in the opposite direction, holding the button in place as you stitch.

5   **Continue until the button is secure**, making sure to stitch through each of the holes in the button, alternating your hole of choice in either a criss-crossing fashion or in parallel stitches.

6   **On the final stitch**, push the needle through the material to the underside of the button. Wrap the thread around the base a few times to secure, then do several anchoring stitches into the fabric.

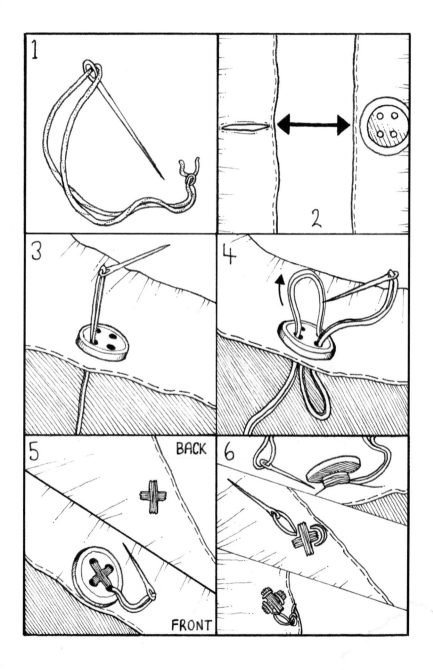

MENDING A SEAM

1   **Rip your clothes.** The first step to adulthood is learning how to fix problems of your own making.

2   **Turn the garment inside out** and find the end of the ripped seam. If there are any loose threads, tie them off to stop the seam from unravelling further.

3   **Thread your needle** with a colour that matches the clothes you've ruined.

4   **To keep your stitch strong**, start sewing about 2 centimetres *before* the hole. Start with a triple stitch by sewing over the top of the same stitch three times to secure.

5   **Make stitching** around half a centimetre in length by dipping your needle through the top side of the fabric, out the bottom and back through, repeating this motion along the seam – this will give your new stitch a little backbone (something you probably can't relate to).

6   **Once you reach the end** of the existing seam, you can begin to mend the actual tear. Using your half-centimetre stitches, join the two sides of the hole together.

7   **Keep sewing** until you hit the intact seam on the other side of the hole, stitching slightly over it as you did in step 4.

8   **Finish with another triple stitch**, then tie a small knot by passing your needle through the loop in your final stitch before pulling it tight. Cut off the remaining thread.

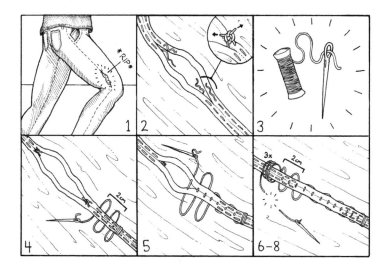

When it comes to sewing, there are a lot of really fancy and important stitches and a million ways to fix broken things, make new things and generally be a sewing superstar. When the weight of your failure to master this essential skill seems almost too much to bear, remember that there's nothing more adult than outsourcing. Act like you know what you're doing and buy a sewing machine or go to a good drycleaner or tailor.

MY PRESENCE IS YOUR PRESENT

Adulting means losing the ability to tag along in whatever group present your mum has organised and paid for. Even more traumatic is the tedious and unnecessary time and effort that goes into wrapping your own gift, only to see your hours of labour torn to shreds by an ungrateful heathen. Save yourself the depression caused by this pointless pursuit with this lazy person's guide to wrapping.

1   **Procure** gift bag.
2   **Place gift** in said bag.
3   **Adorn** with a self-adhesive bow (optional).

> *Some shapes are easier to wrap than others. The best strategy for gift wrapping is to always buy something square. When square gifts are not an option, cheat the system and buy a big square box to cram your misshapen gift in.*
>
> Shit you should know

For those looking for a more sophisticated way to present your present, there is another, more time-consuming way.

1   **Remove the price tags** (unless you bought something really expensive, then leave them on to show people how rich and successful you are).

2   **Unroll your wrapping paper** onto a flat surface. Place the gift in the middle and cut your wrapping paper off from the roll, leaving enough paper to cover both sides of the gift. Leave several centimetres at either end.

3   **Pull the two sides** of the paper taut into the middle of the gift until one edge overlaps the other.

4   **Tape top edge down** to stop paper from flapping all over the place.

5   **Choose an end** and push both sides into the centre, creating 45-degree angles.

6   **Fold the end over** to form a flat edge, then fold it up and tape it to the side of the gift.

7   **Repeat** on the opposite end.

8   **If you're feeling extra fancy**, treat your gift to some stupid shiny ribbon or one of those nifty self-adhesive bows we discussed earlier.

Wrapping anything other than a square is the devil's work and if you're attempting this horrendous task, my thoughts and prayers are with you.

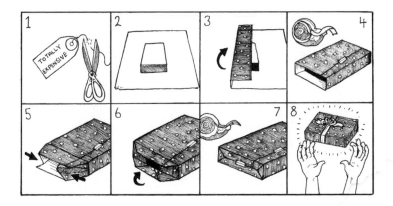

HOW MANY YOUS DOES IT TAKE TO SCREW IN A LIGHT BULB?

Why the fuck are there so many different types of light bulbs? Too many times I have strolled into the grocery store, prepared for the seemingly simple task of choosing a replacement light bulb only to be bombarded with a ridiculous – and frankly, unnecessary – variety of shapes, colour spectrums and fittings that stress me out so badly I want to live in perpetual darkness for the rest of my life.

As it happens, light bulbs have categorising codes (presumably only decipherable by light-bulb creators and/or giant nerds). If you can understand how to decode them, these codes provide an informative guide to the stupid and vast world of lighting. The three different factors used to categorise light bulbs are: shape, base and size.

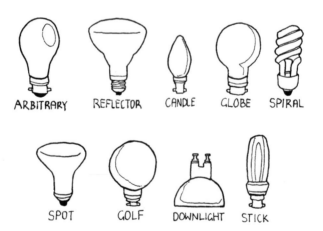

ARBITRARY   REFLECTOR   CANDLE   GLOBE   SPIRAL

SPOT   GOLF   DOWNLIGHT   STICK

GET INTO SHAPE

There are far more shapes of light bulb than what is actually necessary, but apparently each of these funky designs provides a different spread and angle of light. So, if you're looking to spice up your life, why not shake up the light distribution in your house? Go wild, live on the edge, find a new light-bulb shape.

A	**Arbitrary:** *The classic teardrop-shaped bulb, usually fitted to either an Edison screw or bayonet cap base.*
C	**Candle-shaped bulb**
G	**Globular-shaped bulbs**
T	**Tubular lights:** *Typically found in office or industrial buildings. They generally have two pins at either end of the tube.*
R	**Reflector style lamp:** *Dome-shape bulbs which are covered in a reflective material.*

SCREW IT IN (getting to second base)

After you've got the right shape, you need to make sure you get a good screw. Here are the two most common types of light bulb base and their codes.

B (or BC)	**Bayonet cap:** *The standard light-bulb fitting in Australia. It has a cylindrical base with two pins that slip into L-shaped grooves in the socket. These lights use a 'push and twist' action to install.*
E (or ES)	**Edison screw:** *A threaded metal base which screws into the socket. Standard for general-purpose lighting.*

SIZE MATTERS

The numbers that accompany these letter codes are indicative of the distance between the electrical connectors on the base of the bulb, or the width of the lamp itself. Depending on the type of bulb you're using, these measurements can be in millimetres or inches. For general household use, you'd be looking at something around 15 mm in diameter.

On top of shape, base and size, there are a few other factors to help you determine which bulb to buy.

WATTAGE

If you weren't paying attention in high-school science, now is the time for a refresher: a watt is the unit of measurement used for energy. The watt rating on your light bulb refers to the amount of energy consumed by your bulb.

Light bulbs range from 40–120 watts for traditional light fixtures. Using a bulb with a wattage higher than the fixture's capacity is a big fire hazard – however, you can use a bulb with a lower rating than the fixture's requirements.

Just like you, light bulbs are powerful underachievers.

The wattage for your light fixture will be marked on the socket, so always check this before venturing out into the big bright world of light bulbs.

LUMENS

A lumen is how brightness is measured. The more lumens, the closer the appearance to actual sunlight. For example, 400 lumens is the equivalent of a bedside table lamp, and the general recommendation for a living room is 1500 lumens per light.

KELVIN SCALE

The kelvin scale is what bulb colour is measured on. This is how you make sure your bedroom has a sultry orange glow rather than the clinical blue glare of the nursing home you'll be booking yourself into any day now.

1500 K: Orange tones/candlelight glow
2700 K: Yellow spectrum/traditional incandescent bulb
5000 K: Light blue/midday sun
7000 K: Muted blue/overcast sky
10,000 K: Deep blue/evening sky

Shit you should know

Want to know more about light bulbs? WHO DOESN'T? Here are some fun facts about everyone's favourite lighting devices. Make sure to bust these out at your next party!

* *Incandescent bulbs have the shortest life expectancy.*
* *Halogen bulbs are slightly more expensive than incandescent ones, but they're actually cheaper and more efficient over time.*
* *The lifespan of a fluorescent light bulb is significantly lowered the more you turn it off and on.*
* *Only 10% of the energy in an incandescent light bulb is used to create light. The other 90% creates heat.*

Seriously, the list of things you need to know about light bulbs is endless, and it has taken up space in my brain that I'll never get back. Don't memorise this shit, just carry this book around with you until the day you die.

PACKING IT IN: HOW TO TRAVEL LIGHT

It's a general rule of travelling that you must always pack at least four times more undies than you could possibly need, because you never know when you're going to shit yourself multiple times every day of your trip.

In a quest to take smaller bags and still have all the shit you need, here are some tips and tricks to get your bag and life in order:

You'll need to make room for all those underpants by forgetting to pack your toothbrush and socks.

* **Small bag** = less things. Shocker.
* **Use a wheel-less bag**: if you have to carry all your shit, you're a lot more likely to notice how heavy it is and ditch the stuff not worth lugging around.
* **Make a list**; check it twice. Unlike Santa's sack, your list will be filled with the boring adult basics necessary for travel. Any other important packing material should be decided by where you are going and for how long.
  - Toothbrush and paste
  - Deodorant
  - Shoes (and socks)
  - At least one set of clothes and underwear
  - Phone and charger
  - Wallet WITH your ID or passport included – don't be the inconvenient idiot who realises they've left their ID at home in the check-in line.
* **Take multipurpose items**: don't take a different pair of shoes for every day; instead, take some that can be worn for multiple occasions. If you don't have shoes like this, you need to re-evaluate your life choices.

✳ **Wear your bulkiest items** on the plane. The aim is to look bulky and sweaty enough that you get called over for a 'random check' at the security gate.

✳ **Don't pack more** than a week's worth of clothing – if you're gone for longer than that, you should be doing laundry while you're away. You are an adult, after all…

✳ **Make sure everything you pack** matches, especially if you're only taking a limited amount of clothes; give yourself some outfit flexibility in your minimalist wardrobe.

✳ **Choose an e-reader** over books. The most bullshit travelling rule of all. Sadly, books take up a lot of space, and you have to sacrifice some room for all those extra pairs of undies. Really, the only book you'll need to take with you is this one, so I suggest tattooing all my wisdom on your body to save that space.

✳ **Minimise your toiletries**. You're going to forget your toothbrush anyway, so you might as well dispense with the unnecessary one-litre shampoo willingly.

✳ **Put your socks** inside your shoes. In fact, put everything inside everything. Make the inside of your bag like a set of travelling Russian dolls.

✳ **Don't completely** fill your bag. If you have to play Tetris to get your suitcase closed, you've overpacked.

THE INTERNET HAS NO CHILL:
LEAKED NUDES AND SENDING SCREENSHOTS

The internet is the home of the hopeless millennial. Snapchat, Facebook, Instagram and Tinder have brought with them a vast world of online communication. Sadly for us all, social interaction means having to engage with other people – and if there's one thing I know for certain in this world, it's that people are the worst.

The internet has given us a whole mess of new ways to fuck each other over, but while this excessive networking has brought us closer to all the shitty humans we would rather avoid, it's also allowed us to stay connected with the ones we actually like. It's a fifty–fifty split between horrible social interaction and an endless stream of memes shared between friends on a half-hourly basis. Luckily, my meme-sharing gang of fellow hopeless millennials provided the perfect sounding-board for all problems both online and IRL, and their wisdom offers solutions to every issue caused by human interaction.

LEAKED NUDES

The biggest fear of modern dating. Leaked nudes and revenge porn are very real and scary things. If we're being honest, people care a lot less about seeing your bits than they do about seeing someone famous, but that doesn't mean having your nudes leaked isn't still one of the shittiest possible outcomes of sending a rogue nip-shot on Snapchat.

As per the wisdom of the millennial meme-committee, there are three plausible solutions to the dreaded nude leak.

✳ **Report it:** Anyone who leaks nudes is an arsehole. There's no two ways about it. No excuse or reasoning is adequate validation for breaking someone's trust. But most importantly, leaking nudes is actually a crime. If your nudes are leaked, the first step is to take screenshots. Try to capture every place the photos have gone, and the conversations they were initially sent in, then go to the cops. Give them as much information as you can about the shithead who fucked you over and let them get fucked over right back.

✳ **In Kardashian we trust:** The worst has happened and, I'm not going to lie, it's going to be a pretty shit time. But every cloud has a silver lining; look at Kimmy K – she rode that nudity success train all the way to Hollywood, and took her whole family along with her. Everyone has a body, and yours is clearly fresh enough that people want to have a good look, whether they're willing to admit it or not. Own it, work it, and fuck the haters.

✳ **Social detox:** Running away from a problem generally isn't a sustainable solution, but we all know social media can be pretty toxic. Take a step back, do a clear-out of your profiles, cull your friends and photos and update your privacy settings. Then maybe buy a ticket to Europe and drown yourself in bottomless mimosas until it all blows over...

SENDING SCREENSHOTS

Is there anything more cathartic than sending screenshots of an argument to your mates and having a bitch-and-response session? Probably, but I don't want to hear about it… Despite the therapeutic benefits, sending screenshots is a risky business. The possibility of accidentally sending your shot to the screenshotee themselves is all too real. Luckily, trial, error and squad wisdom have yielded three solutions to this anxiety-riddled scenario.

* **Deflection:** They've received the screenshot; those three little dots have popped up; a response is imminent…
  'Did you just screenshot our convo to send to someone else?'
  'No, I just didn't understand what you meant here. Can you please explain?'
  Deflected. You know you're lying, they know you're lying, but no one wants to be the one to call bullshit.

* **Own it:** Assume that everything you say is going to be heard by more than one person, so say what you mean and be willing to stand behind it. The same rule applies to screenshots. If you're going to send one on, there's a chance you're going to get caught out, so be prepared to stand up, face the music and deal with it – just like a real grown-up.

* **Butterfly effect:** It's a bit of a cop-out, but the best solution is to not send the screenshot to begin with. Duh. Go back in time and stop yourself from taking it. Or, even better, just discuss the issue with the person you're talking to from the outset. Confrontation is the worst, but doing shitty, unpleasant things is basically the definition of adulthood.

HELPFUL
TIPS FOR
ADULT
PROFESSIONALISM

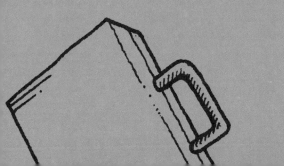

THE ADULT WORLD is filled with many terrifying things but finding and keeping a job may be the most stressful of them all. Resumes and cover letters are only the first step into this baffling and exhausting land of professionalism. Once you've prepared these, you'll then have to actually interact with other humans, present yourself well, be capable of conducting real conversations in which you make statements and have opinions, and perform a function other than sitting in a dark, gungy room playing PlayStation for hours on end. Luckily, this hopeless millennial has the hook-ups with real-life adults who have been doing this employment thing for longer than I've been alive. So chill: these tips for becoming a sweet professional have been tried and tested by actual grown-ups with proper jobs, money and super funds.

DOCUMENTS DETAILING YOUR FALSIFIED USEFULNESS: WRITING A RESUME

A resume (also known as a *curriculum vitae*, in case you want to look cultured and shit) is the first building block to hooking yourself up with a job/money/financial security/crushing adult responsibility. Resumes are really just professional bios that give you a soapbox through which to yell about how great and worthy of a regular pay check you are. They're the first impression a potential employer gets of you, and a good opportunity to tell people about all your accomplishments that are too awkward to bring up in conversation.

IT'S NOT ALL ABOUT YOU

One of the biggest mistakes people make when writing their resumes is oversharing. Millennials have a propensity for thinking they're the greatest thing since sliced bread (I mean, obvs, everything we do is total fire). If possible, resumes should only be about a page in length; you know you're a special little sunflower who is obviously perfect for whatever job you're applying for, but the remainder of the population isn't clued in yet, and there will be many others also living with the belief that the Earth revolves around them who have applied for the same position. Have some compassion for whoever is reading the vast expanse of resumes flooding in, and give them something light, pithy and informative. But, while it's important to keep your resume tight, there are a few key points that can't be avoided.

* **The essentials:** Your name, address, contact details and date of birth.
* **Overview statement:** Herein lies the perfect place

to word-vomit about how great you are. This section should be about a paragraph in length and showcase who you are and why you're applying for the job.

✳ **Qualifications, degrees and skills:** Include any learnings, courses or knowledge you have that contribute to your ability to perform the job. It's also worth including something that shows you are dedicated and persistent. If you have an arts degree in philosophy, that expensive piece of paper will really only be good for showing potential employers that, despite your poor decision-making skills, you're diligent when it comes to hard (and pointless) tasks.

Sadly, an extended diatribe about your ATAR, the sports you played when you were nine and a comprehensive overview of all your hobbies is not something your future employer gives two shits about.

✳ **Experience:** This is the space to list your previous jobs and internships, and explain the roles and responsibilities you undertook there. Here, you must remember the golden rule of resumes: short and sweet. Only include the most recent and relevant positions you've held. Working at KFC for two years in high school, while being a sad and depressing time for you, is not relevant to anyone else, unless you're vying for a job at the Fried Chicken Headquarters and they're desperate to get their hands on that secret recipe.

✳ **Key strengths:** What are you good at? Probably not much if you need this book... Regardless, in this section it's important to dig deep and at least attempt to make yourself sound like a functioning human adult. Try to relate your key strengths to the role you're applying for. There are some skills – like organisation and working within a team – that are generally relevant to any role; however, try to keep in mind that you're never going to be the only person applying for a job, so while it's important to be truthful in your resume, you need to highlight the things that are unique and interesting about yourself. What is it that you can bring to this role that nobody else can?

✳ **Interests:** While I would definitely not recommend including an entire section about how much you love getting munted at music festivals, you should add a bit of information about things you enjoy doing outside of the workplace to help make you seem like a well-rounded individual – your true level of trash-baggery can stay a little secret between you and me.

✳ **References:** Try to find at least 2–3 people who don't think you're a total trash bag and might be persuaded to say something vaguely positive about your work ethic and general character. Include their best contact details and make a small note that these referees are willing to talk if contacted (be sure to confirm this with the referees first; there's nothing worse than a referee who tells everyone you're the fucking worst and gave out their number without permission).

RESEARCH RATHER RELUCTANTLY

The other most important element of writing a resume is research. It's important to keep in mind what type of job you're applying for, and what the employers at this company will be looking for in their applicants. Yes, this requires more work and means that submitting your resume cannot be done in the classic copy-and-paste style. Strangely enough, putting in a sliver of effort with your application will provide you with a couple of benefits.

* **Firstly:** Whoever you're submitting your resume to is getting a more personalised document that shows you're willing to put in some semblance of work and commitment.

* **Secondly:** The research and extra work will help make sure you're applying for a job that actually interests and engages you. I know the idea of fulfilling employment is a pretty foreign concept to most of you, but it's really not so far out of the realm of possibility, and by fully understanding and appreciating the job you're applying for, you're one step closer to doing something that doesn't make you want to blow your brains out.

COVER YOUR LETTER
(AND YOURSELF)

A cover letter is a fundamental addition to every successful job application. Some employers won't even consider your application without one. While your resume is the place to highlight all the necessary information someone needs to hire you, your cover letter is where you can show a little more of your personality, as well as all that research we talked about earlier.

Like your resume, your cover letter shouldn't be overly long; aim for about a page of self-love and ramblings, all the while trying to include these things.

* **The recipient:** Who is this cover letter going to? Try to make it personal and actually address the person you're writing to. If that information isn't available, keep it professional and go for the generic 'Dear Sir/Madam', or 'To Whom it May Concern'.

* **What are you applying for?** Before you even begin your application, include a line at the beginning that references the position you're applying for, for example: Re: Application for Potential Income Which Will Keep Me from the Brink of Death and Destitution.

* **Run-down:** Give a brief overview of who you are and what you're about. Keep in mind that the recipient will be reading your cover letter alongside your resume, so try not to repeat everything word for word. That being said, you should refer to your attached resume and briefly emphasise some of your key skills and relevant experience.

* **Job listing:** Mention where you saw the job advertised, or how you heard about it. In addition to that, suck up just a smidge and let the employer know why the job appeals to you – probably work something in

about how it appeals to your skills and experience, not the fact that you're desperate for money and will do anything for that cold hard cash.

* **RESEARCH!** Again, research is so important in giving the false impression that you actually have a brain in your skull and something resembling a work ethic. Show that you understand the role and the company, and that this isn't some blanket job application. Make them see you're enthused about the job and excited about the possibility of working there.

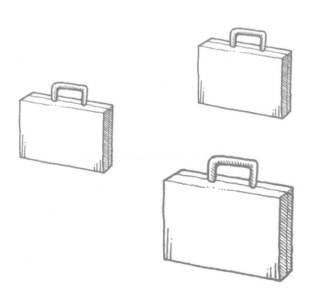

TIPS FOR AWKWARD CONVERSATIONS ABOUT RAISES AND PROMOTIONS

Money: aka the root of all evil; aka the thing I crave most in this sad, disappointing world. While having a job you genuinely love and enjoy is an absolute blessing, an even bigger blessing is having a job that you genuinely love and enjoy which pays you huge sacks of cash and maybe gives you a gold-plated Tesla or a helicopter or something.

Everyone wants a promotion or a raise – it's the way of life; humans are constantly vying for more. But the fact is, sometimes we don't deserve them, or it's simply not the right time. The unavoidable truth of the situation is that if you want a raise or promotion, you're most likely going to have to ask for one. And let's be real: having a conversation with anyone about anything other than the weather is a real bloody hassle and probably not worth it if I'm honest.

In some lucky circumstances, your boss may approach you to offer you a raise or promotion, but chances are you're going to have to champion yourself and start that professional conversation on your own, buddy.

Employers generally have a lot more on their plates than thinking about the salary of just one employee.

While the standard of your work is perhaps the most important element in securing a raise, there are a couple of other factors that come into play when a pay increase is being considered by an employer.

* **The market:** You're a real adult now, and that means you have to care about things like the economy, your industry and exchange rates.
* **How the business itself is doing:** Did your company just lay off ten people? Have there been loud, scary conversations in your boss's office where the phrase 'The sky is falling' was yelled in hysterical tones?

It seems pretty self-explanatory that if there's been a big financial event, like the GFC, or your company has just lost a major shareholder or client, there are probably some difficult financial times going on for your employer. A good rule of thumb for approaching your boss about a pay rise is to be considerate and informed (in fact, this is just a good approach to life in general. Don't be a dick; know what you're talking about; make the world a better place. Easy).

Another important consideration is your company's policy on pay rises. In fact, this is something you should know about before you take a job. If getting a pay rise annually is going to make or break a position for you, you need to have that conversation before you sign the contract. If you're unsure what the company policy is, ask the HR department. The same goes for promotions. While these things should realistically be based on merit, some companies' policies are based on more tangible time frames or KPIs, so knowing the parameters around those, and working towards achieving them, will back up your request for a raise or promotion.

HAVING 'THE TALK'

Once you've assessed the variety of factors that contribute to the timing of a raise or promotion, there are three easy steps to approach asking for your raise – and when I say 'easy', I'm trying to lull you into a false sense of security; this convo is going to be hella awkward and uncomfortable and there's absolutely no way around that, soz.

* **Email:** Send your boss an email to let them know you'd like to discuss the possibility of a raise or promotion. The purpose of this email is twofold:
    - The first reason is so your request is in writing. This way there's a clear timeline from the point when you first asked for a raise, which means if you aren't successful this time, your boss can look back in the future and acknowledge that you have been patiently waiting for a raise since your last request.
    - The second reason is that this email gives you a chance to accumulate and document all the reasons why you deserve a raise. You're giving yourself a stress-free environment in which to put together an overview of your successes and the standard of your work – a self-evaluation that will be necessary when you actually sit down face to face with your boss. This is your homework; don't slack off.

✳   **Talk:** When you get to the point of sitting down with your boss to discuss your request, you'll need to present your reasoning for why you deserve more money. Your email was just an introduction to all the reasons why you're so great and need enough money to buy a boat – you really need to show your worth here. I'm sure that, for you, finding examples of why you're a decent employee will be quite a task, but talking about successful projects you've worked on, times you've used your initiative to improve something about your office, or mentioning some external work, course or research you've done to improve your performance are good places to start.

✳   **Negotiate:** Know how much you want your pay to increase, then ask for a fraction more; that way you have a small bargaining chip if they're not able, or ready, to give you that higher amount.

While these tips and pointers are important for getting you into a conversation about money with your employer, they do not guarantee you will actually get a raise or promotion. There's an overriding message to the life lessons in this book: hope for the best and prepare for the worst. You can be the best employee in the world, but if your company is not in the financial state to give you a raise, you can hardly expect one.

FOOL PEOPLE WITH A GOOD FIRST IMPRESSION

A good first impression is the essential ingredient for creating an image of yourself as a high-functioning adult. Make someone think you have it together when you first meet and it will take years of poor decision-making and general jack-arsery for them to realise you're actually a trash bag. Who knows; maybe by the time that first impression has worn off, you'll have become the person you were pretending to be – it's nice to have dreams.

The unfortunate truth of this world is that some people are just better than others. We like to pretend there's an even playing field, but let's be real: we all have that one friend who's annoyingly good at living and we can't understand why. Usually, these people have a few defining characteristics: they're chatty, gregarious, friendly and level-headed. For those of us not gifted with these traits, the key is to fake it 'til you make it. And you can curate this image with only a slight outpouring of effort on your behalf.

* **Avoid nudity:** It goes without saying that wearing that trashy Bintang singlet you've been sleeping in for the last five years is not going to help you out in the professional world, or even the regular world; you look like a class-A bogan and no one is digging it…
* **Don't be a dick:** Be polite. This is actually not that fucking hard. Please; thank you; smile. Simple. Good manners should not be reserved just for making good impressions.
* **What's in a name?** Remembering names is one of the hardest tasks known to man, but it's a skill that goes an extraordinarily long way when making first impressions.

When someone introduces themselves, look them in the eye and repeat, 'It's nice to meet you, Carl.' I know it will be hard for you, but try to do this in the least creepy way possible. If you get really stuck on someone's name, relate it to some redeeming feature about them. For example, Carl looks like a cow. Carl; cow. Now every time you think, *God, that man looks like a delicious meaty snack* you'll immediately think: *Carl*. Voila.

* **Body language:** Unfortunately for the awkward population of the planet, eye contact is a cornerstone of being a polite adult. Look at someone while they're talking to you, and when you're answering a question, look directly into the speaker's eyes. While you're staring deep into the baby-blues of your interviewer, your nerves are likely to be out of control, and fidgeting is the natural result. Alas, this is a sure-fire way to clue people in to the fact you are absolutely shitting bricks and can't wait to get home and watch Netflix in your underpants. Try to compose yourself and keep still; don't cross your arms and legs. If you're really struggling, put your hands on your knees and try to open up your chest – this will help you breathe deeply, which will calm you.

  > Eye contact: Like any form of human connection, this is awkward as fuck. Nobody wants to make extended eye contact – it's creepy and weird.

* **Breathe:** This might sound ridiculously obvious, but breathing is the key to calming your nerves and staying alive and shit. It's easy to fuck up a first impression when you can't stop fidgeting and can barely comprehend what you're saying because you're so nervous. Take a second, breathe deep, get your

shit together; it's natural to be nervous. When making a first impression, you're on show, so go with it! Give them a performance they won't forget – preferably by being impressive, not by vomiting on yourself in a fit of anxiety… But hey, to each their own.

✳ **Social media:** In these terrifying modern times, social media forms more of a pre-impression than a first impression. That scary speech they used to give you in school about everything you put on the internet haunting you through the ghostly wires of the web forever is unfortunately true. The first thing that most humans do – whether they be employers, Tinder dates or other – before meeting someone is look them up on the interweb. If your Facebook is 60% photos of you pissed beyond comprehension in some backwater club, 30% statuses about how much you love smoking pot instead of working, and 10% *Simpsons* memes nobody gets anymore, then you might need to re-evaluate your online presence – or at least change your privacy settings… While there are many, many negatives to your trashy internet footprint, there are some positives too! Having a LinkedIn profile that engages with your chosen industry is one way to show you're serious and committed to whatever field you're in. It's also a great way to stalk others at your level and see how much better they're doing at life than you.

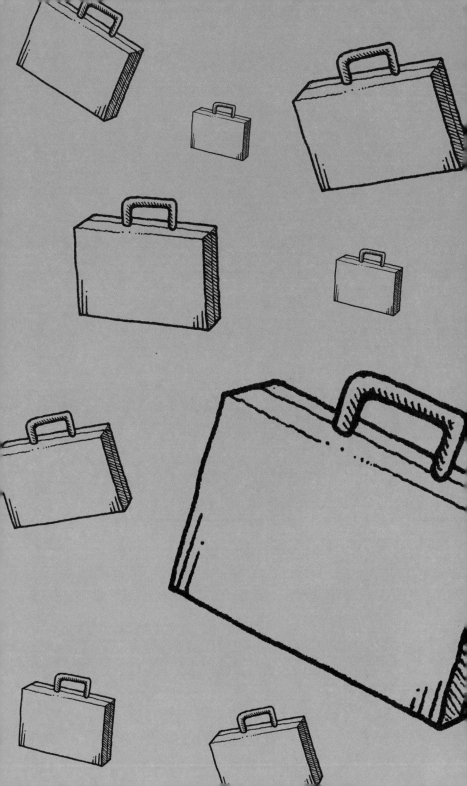

WEARING PANTS AND OTHER PROFESSIONAL ATTIRE

We all like to pretend that how we dress doesn't really influence our lives that much, but the truth of the matter is that you are like a little present, and your clothes are the wrapping. If you're covered in shitty old newspaper that's barely held together with masking tape, you're just not going to be as appealing as that big shiny box with the curled ribbon, ya feel?

Dressing well for an interview, the first day on the job, or an important meeting shows respect for the people you're engaging with. Every human knows how much of a hassle it is to put in effort, which means we can all appreciate a bit of work when we see it.

Unfortunately, the standards of dress vary dramatically from place to place, so making hard and fast rules about what you should and shouldn't wear is almost impossible. Regardless, there are things you can do to ensure you're putting your best foot forward, and wearing something other than that pair of Vans that have seen better days is a good place to start.

* **Plan ahead:** Find out the dress code before you arrive. This can take out a huge amount of the anxiety around dressing for any occasion. My mum always told me to 'dress up, not down', but there's little more embarrassing than turning up in a ballgown when everyone else is in boardies and thongs.

* **Be sensible and practical:** If you can't figure out the dress code, go with something smart-casual (i.e. 'smasual') and practical. There's not much that can go wrong with a clean blouse/shirt and some matching pants (i.e. 'jeans and a nice top').

✳   **Be yourself!** Just because you have to follow certain standards for how you dress, doesn't mean you should hide your personality. If you love wearing bright colours and fun socks, then go for it! Although interviews are about presenting yourself as well as you can, it's still about you; no one wants a job they had to pretend to be someone else to get.

If you have an interview or important event coming up, figure out what you're going to wear the night before. Don't leave it to the morning of and get stuck digging your dirty, beer-stained chinos from the bottom of your washing basket, you filthy animal.

Shit you should know

Despite what we've been told most of our lives through film, books, music and every generation that's come before, it is possible to have a job you love that inspires you to work hard and enjoy yourself while you do it. I've been #blessed in my working life thus far, but there is no way this luck or passion is limited to me. One of the driving factors behind working in a job you love and that fulfils you is the freedom to be yourself and share your interests within your workplace. If this means showing your dope-ass tattoos, flashing a shiny septum piercing or wearing a technicolour dreamcoat to work, fucking go for it. You do you, be free and be happy, because these are the things that make you work well and work hard. Inspirational workplace rant over. Go get paid.

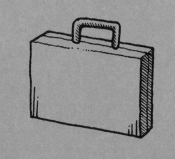

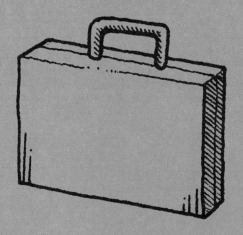

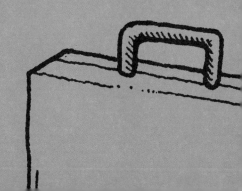

TIES: JUST SCARVES TIED WITH MORE HAND-EYE COORDINATION?

I'm pretty sure ties are a relic of generations past. The last time I saw someone wearing a tie was at a funeral, so I'm sure I can be excused for thinking they are probably the most depressing accessory in the history of the universe. That being said, I work in the most casual office in the world and turning up in a tie would probably be seen more as off-putting than professional. But I'm sure there are some horribly sad and uncomfortable millennial finance bros out there who are tired of wearing clip-on ties to work. This one's for you.

1   **Procure tie** and collared shirt.

2   **Put the wide end of the tie on the right** and the small end on the left. The tip of the wide end should hang a lot lower than the small.

3   **Put the wide end over the small end**, bring it behind and around, then up through the loop around your neck.

4   **Bring the wide end down to the right**, then take it to the left underneath the small end.

5   **Pull the wide end up** and bring it down again through the neck loop to the right-hand side.

6   **Take the wide end over the top** of the knot to the left, then bring it up through the neck loop once again.

7   **Pull the wide end down** through the loop you've
    just created.

8   **Tighten** by pulling down on the small end and slipping
    the knot up.

If you're as confused by those instructions as I am, pretend you're
looking in a mirror and use this diagram as a guide.

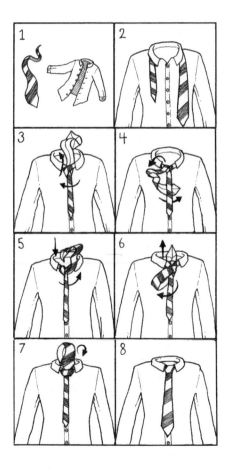

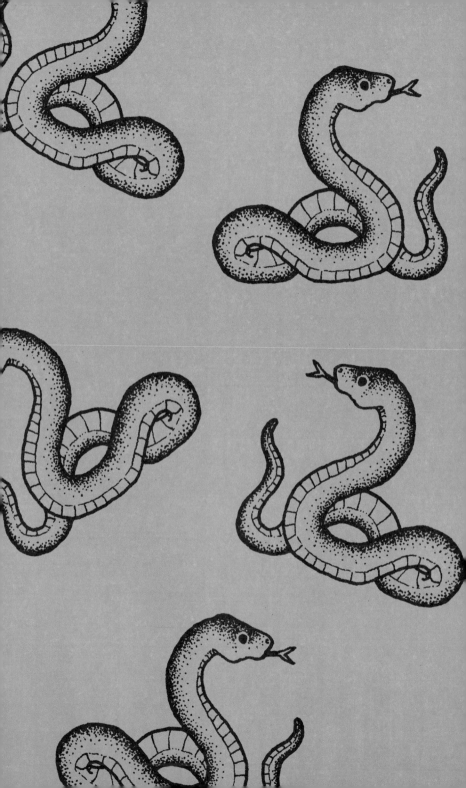

HOW
NOT TO
DIE IN THE
WILDERNESS

THE WILDERNESS: it's dirty, filled with bugs and animals that probably want to eat you, lay eggs in you, or generally fuck with you in some horrifying and bizarre manner. Surviving in the outdoor world requires a skill set that I unfortunately do not possess. The chance of falling into a deep hole filled with snakes, disappearing into a pit of quicksand, or dying of dehydration 10 metres from clean water are all very real and fearsome possibilities. To alleviate my outdoor helplessness, I called on the help of a man whose talent at fire-building is unsurpassed, and who could survive better in the wilderness blindfolded and missing a leg than I can in my own home – and he would know, because he's my housemate…

DUMPSTER FIRE (YOU'RE THE DUMPSTER, I'M THE FIRE)

Fire. Man makes it. It's essentially our evolutionary legacy. Without it, we're just smelly cave people, eating berries and waiting for winter to bring us hypothermia and starvation. If you want to call yourself a real human adult, it's time to start playing with fire.

Building your fire is like building a tiny house; a tiny house that you're about the reduce to a smouldering pile of embers.

WOODS TO BURN	WOODS TO AVOID
Ironbark	Green wood
Boxwood	Soft woods, e.g. pine
River red gum	Driftwood (the dried salt in it can release a harmful chemical as it burns)
Eucalyptus	Any poisonous trees or plants like oleander

If you keep your bigger pieces of wood around the fire (note: around, not inside), it will help dry them out and make them burn better later.

Shit you should know

What You'll Need

LIGHTER OR MATCHES

ROCKS

TINDER (NOT THE APP, IDIOT): LIGHT, DRY WEEDS AND BARK; SMALL STICKS

KINDLING: DRY STICKS AND BRANCHES (you can tell the branches are dry if they snap audibly)

A MEDIUM-SIZED STICK WITH A Y-POINT, AND A STRAIGHT STICK ABOUT THE SAME SIZE (if you can't find one, don't panic. This shape helps to create the teepee for your fire, but isn't 100% necessary)

BIGGER WOOD: you'll find the best pieces of wood fresh on the ground, just make sure they're dry!

1. Dig a hole as shallow as you are and create a windbreaker around it using rocks.
2. Swipe some tinder right into the centre of your firepit.
3. Make a little teepee on top of the tinder using your kindling and Y-point stick, adding more kindling around your structure. Keep a small opening in the teepee through which to light your fire.
4. Light your tinder, and gently blow across to fan the flames.
5. As the fire grows, slowly fuel it with more kindling. Avoid putting the kindling directly on top of your fire, but instead stack it carefully to ensure adequate airflow.
6. As the flames continue to grow, add bigger pieces of wood to the fire.

HOW NOT TO RELIVE
THE BLAIR WITCH PROJECT

Don't get lost. Don't follow strangers deep into the forest.
If you see creepy, demonic dolls hanging from trees, run in the
other direction.

Before you even start your outdoor adventure, you should
always have a general idea of your surroundings. Take note:

* ✳ **What's around you?**
* ✳ **How big is the bush**/forest/walking track you're about
  to embark on?
* ✳ **Is there water** nearby?
* ✳ **Has there been** a series of mysteriously unexplained
  disappearances in the area?
* ✳ **Do local children** tell urban legends about a witch who
  steals your soul?
* ✳ **Do locals avoid** the area at night?
* ✳ **Do you know how to use the sun** to navigate? That
  big ball of gas rises in the east and sets in the west.
  If you know what direction home is, the sun will help
  you find it.
* ✳ **If night falls** and you're completely lost, build a fire
  and stay put! If you know people are searching for you,
  build a fire with green wood to make a smoky signal.
* ✳ **Head for higher ground** and try to find a vantage point.
* ✳ **If you're near the ocean**, try to find a beach. Coastline
  generally equals humans (or else you'll stumble on
  some *Lord of the Flies* society of barbaric children;
  it's a fifty–fifty chance).

YOU KNOW NORTH-ING:
FINDING NORTH

Directions: my knowledge of them extends from left to right, and sometimes that's too much for me. Anything more delves into the territory of information that is too practical for my tiny brain. Even if I were to know how to find north, it would be no help as I generally have no idea which direction I'm meant to be going anyway. However, I am painfully aware that there are many, many people less directionally challenged than myself, and I want to pretend to be as smart as them.

* **A watch:** I know, I know, it's 2020 and watches have been made redundant by the technological revolution. Luckily for us, hipsters exist, and we all know hipsters love nothing more than old, pointless technology, including, but not limited to, analogue watches.
  - Point the hour hand of your watch towards the sun.
  - The midway point between the twelve o'clock position and the hour hand is south. North is opposite south.
* **The sun:** If you were paying attention, you'd know by now that the sun rises in the east and sets in the west. By a process of elimination, you should be able to find north (I'm probably putting a little too much faith in you with that assumption: prove me wrong).
* **Stars:** Unsurprisingly, a constellation that is literally named after a point on the compass is going to help you find north.

The Southern Cross is the most recognisable constellation in the Southern Hemisphere. It's made up of five stars: Alpha, Beta, Gamma, Delta, and Epsilon Crucis. There are two pointer stars (Alpha and Beta Centauri) that point to the top star in the Southern Cross.

Shit you should know

1   Locate the Southern Cross.

2   Find the two stars that form the longest axis of the constellation. These stars make an arrow that points towards the south pole.

3   Follow the line of the stars downwards by five times the distance between the stars themselves.

4   Draw an imaginary line from this point to the ground, this is true south, making true north directly behind you.

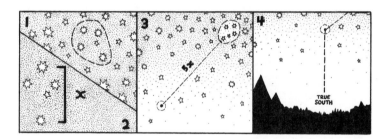

SHELTER FROM THE STORM

Despite all my wonderful navigational advice and tips for escaping the Blair Witch, if you're as hopeless as I assume you are, it's pretty likely you're still going to get lost in the wilderness anyway. If you're trapped in that scary outside world with no chance of finding your way home, your best bet is to find shelter until someone realises you're missing and comes to find you, or you get eaten by a bear.

* **Stay dry:** The best shelter is dry shelter. You want to set up camp in the driest place you can find.
* **High ground:** If you can, make your shelter on higher ground; this will give you a better vantage point. Keep in mind that you shouldn't stray too far from your original path – the further astray you go, the harder you'll be to find.
* **Fallen trees:** Nature's pre-made shelter. If you have a tarp, you can drape this over a tree to make shelter, or if it's dry and leafy enough, you can use the canopy of the fallen tree itself. Moral of this story: always bring a tarp.
* **Leaves:** Dry leaves are the heart and soul of your shelter. They'll form the perfect bed, blanket and companion for your dark and lonely nights.
* **Rocks:** Try to find naturally formed shelters, like natural rock formations. Bear in mind that there might already be other creatures who had the same idea as you; snakes and shit are terrifying enough from a distance, even worse once you've pissed them off by putting your giant feet in their house, so watch your step.
* **Avoid:**
  - Wet ground and anywhere next to moving water.
  - Exposed, open ridges.
  - Building in the heat of the day – this will just exhaust and dehydrate you.

It probably goes without saying that the biggest tip for surviving in the outside world is preparation. Always tell someone where you're going and how long you expect to be gone. Bring all the supplies you need with you, plus a little extra. Know your surroundings and have a general idea of where you're going. And most of all, don't be stupid.

Shit you should know

If you're going bushwalking or wilderness exploring, always take a small survival kit, including:

* *Water – so much water*
* *Food that won't go off*
* *First-aid supplies*
* *A torch*
* *A small tarp or waterproof sheet*
* *Matches or a lighter*
* *A portable battery-operated radio*
* *A knife*

FISHING: FOR MORE THAN JUST COMPLIMENTS

There's only so long you can survive in the wilderness on a diet of leaves and suspect mushrooms. While having to catch and kill your own food is something you will hopefully never need to do, it's nice to have a lot of useless knowledge that makes it seem like you know shit about being alive. Plus, you never know when that lie you told your Tinder date about being 'really outdoorsy' will bite you in the arse and force you to actually go outside and camp.

What You'll Need

A FISHING ROD AND LINE

SINKERS: *These lower your line further into the water; the deeper your line goes, the more likely you are to catch something.*

HOOKS

FLOATS: *These let you know when fish are biting as the float bobs up and down in the water.*

BAIT: *Fish eat a lot of random stuff; bait can be anything from worms or cheese to bits of other fish. Different fish eat different things, so the more advanced you become, the more research you need to put into your bait.*

A KNIFE

PLIERS TO REMOVE HOOK

A FISHING LICENCE: *This can depend on which state you're in, but as usual the internet has all the answers, so check the Department of Agriculture website for more info.*

WHERE THE FISH AT?

For a beginner, the easiest place to fish is a still body of water. This would preferably be a location you know to have fish in it, like a lake or dam, not your overflowing bathtub.

The best areas will have sand and a weedy shore, and although fish tend to hang around rocky areas, it's good to avoid these if you're a beginner – getting your line snagged in rocks is not a fun time.

TO BOAT OR NOT TO BOAT?

While it is possible to fish from the shore, the deeper and closer to a current you go, the more chances you have of finding fish. Grab yourself a boat, kayak or curvy piece of driftwood to fish from and go wild!

FISH WEAR WATCHES TOO

Dusk and dawn are the prime times for finding fish; it's when they're most active and likely to come out of their little fish houses to be caught.

GET YOUR SHIT TOGETHER

As it turns out, you can buy lightweight fishing rods that come with pre-spooled lines. These are generally sold for children, but given your extreme lack of life ability I think you would easily fit into this category.

Once you've got a hold of your child-rod (or stick with string tied to the end), attach your bait to the hook. You can use fresh bait, like worms, or something frozen, like squid. You can also use cheese, bread or plastic baits.

CAST AWAY

After you've set up your assorted fishing stuff you can cast your line.

1. **Face the direction** where all the fish be chillin' and make sure no one's standing behind you – snagging someone's face on your line is not a good way to make friends.

2. **Leave about 30 centimetres** hanging from the end of the line, with your floater or bait dangling from the end.

3. **Holding the rod with both hands,** raise your dominant hand until your arm is in front of your face so the rod is pointing slightly behind you.

4. **Flick the rod** forward in one swift, fluid motion and pray it reaches the spot you were aiming for.

5. **Once your line is out** there, the fish have got to come to you. If you hook one, you'll feel a tug on the line – play it cool and reel it in slowly.

6. **This is where we hit** the 'choose your own adventure' section of your outdoor experience: free the fish or go full wild and eat it.

FISH ARE FRIENDS

Personally, if I were lost in the wilderness and there was a choice between eating the possibly hallucinogenic/poisonous mushrooms, or catching, killing and eating a fish, I'd pick the shrooms. But I promised you a Bear Grylls style guide to surviving (but definitely not thriving) in the wilderness, so here we go.

1   **You've caught the fish.** This is the point where you can still turn back and release Nemo into the ocean to join his fishy comrades.

2   **Regardless of whether** you're going to eat it or not, you'll need to unhook the fish from your line. Use pliers to grip the hook, then gently and slowly rotate the hook and pull it back out the way it went in. If the fish doesn't have teeth, you can use your fingers to do this, although I can guarantee that no fish is going to enjoy you sticking your dirty fingers in its mouth. Throw your fish back in the water, or read on.

3   **The fish's fate** is decided; I guess you didn't catch it for nothing. If you're going to eat your fish, you need to kill it as quickly and humanely as possible. This is where things get a little graphic, so look away now if you're not down for the icky stuff.

4   **You need to kill the fish** as soon as you can after you've caught it. Percussive trauma is generally accepted as the most humane method of killing a fish. This is basically where you give a forceful and swift blow to the fish's head, just above the eyes. It's going to be intense, but you need to be as deliberate and firm as possible – the more hesitant you are, the more likely it is you'll just stun and hurt the fish rather than killing it.

5   **If you have a scaling knife**, you can remove the scales by scraping from tail to head. Otherwise, remove the skin.

6   **If you thought the worst was over**, you were dead
     wrong, just like the fish… Too soon? The next step
     is to clean and gut the fish. To do this, you'll need to
     insert your knife into the fish's anus and slice upwards
     through to the gills. The only redeeming part of these
     instructions is that I've said anus, twice.

7   **Remove the fish's innards**, and rinse thoroughly.

8   **Get a fire going**, cook the fish and eat it. This
     horrendous task is done; I hope that fish was delicious.

There you have it, the traumatic art of fishing. Turns out it's less
pleasantly floating down the river and more predator-eats-prey
than I had anticipated… Let's never go outside again.

Shit you should know

*There are regulations around catching fish, and a licence
may be needed. Make sure you check the size and species
of your fish with your state's requirements before stuffing it
in your face. If your fish doesn't stack up, throw it back and
try again.*

LET IT RIP: ESCAPING RIP CURRENTS (AND RESPONSIBILITY)

The ocean is filled with a lot of scary shit. There's a whole mess of stuff deep down in those watery depths that we're all better off ignoring (until they rise up and chomp down on our slippery, sunburnt bodies).

It's hard to think of anything more dangerous than prehistoric aquatic monsters and sharks bigger than Tasmania, but the fact is, the scariest thing about the ocean is the ocean itself. Rip currents are one of the biggest hazards for ocean swimmers. It's more likely that you'll be pulled out to sea by a rip than a toothy shark any day.

When a wave breaks, the water pushed to the shore needs to find a way back to the ocean. The water flows through the channels of the shoreline and back to sea, creating a rip current.

Although rips can be difficult to spot, there are some general characteristics to look out for:

* **Deeper**, darker water
* **Fewer** breaking waves
* **Rippled** surface surrounded by still water
* **Ocean gunk** floating at the back of the waves

If you miss the signs and happen to be caught up in a rip, there are a few things you can do to get out of it.

✳ **Stay calm** – panicking and flailing around is only going to wear you out.

✳ **Don't try** to swim against the rip; the ocean is a lot stronger than you are.

✳ **Float** to conserve your energy.

✳ **Raise your arm** to signal for help. Funnily enough, there are people whose job it is to save you from the terrors of the ocean – lifesavers are there to help.

✳ **If you can**, swim parallel to the beach towards the breaking waves.

CLIMB AWAY FROM YOUR PROBLEMS: TREE CLIMBING FOR HUMANS

Like humans, trees come in many shapes and sizes. While this abundance of trees means there is almost unlimited potential for unique climbing experiences, it also means some trees were just not built for climbing. Learn to find the perfect tree to climb and you'll always have somewhere to hide away when being an adult becomes too much.

* **Know your ability**: Look, if you're reading a guide on how to climb a tree, chances are you don't have a lot of natural talent. Be realistic in your climbing endeavours.
* **Not all trees** were created equal: Pick the right tree for your climbing needs.
  - Find one big enough to provide you with all the stability you've been missing from your life thus far.
  - Look for low-hanging branches.
  - Is the tree leafy? If it's completely bare, that probably means it's as dead as you are inside, and far more likely to break under the weight of your many, many insecurities.
  - If there are white ants or termites, do not climb.

WHAT TO DO

* **Put all your weight** as close to the trunk as possible.
* **Test each branch** before you climb on it.
* **While society at large** would probably prosper from you being trapped in a tree forever, make sure you check your distance from the ground and don't go higher than you're comfortable with. This will make returning to ground level a much less daunting process.
* **What comes up** must come down – make sure you have an exit path.
* **If you have to jump down**, make sure to roll when you hit the ground.
* **Wear shoes**, preferably something more supportive than thongs.
* **Don't fall**.

IT'S TICKING ME OFF (BECAUSE IT'S A FUCKING GROSS BUG)

The outdoors is full of a lot of shit that wants to do you harm, especially if you live in Australia. In fact, there are animals, insects and plants that exist for the sole purpose of fucking you up everywhere in this bloody country. Death is the only true escape. Let the flora and fauna have their way with you and be done with it. But if for some reason the idea of tiny bugs sucking all your fluids out of you and leaving you to die on the forest floor doesn't appeal to you, read on.

Ticks are parasites that need blood to grow and have no hesitation feeding off you to get it. One of the most common bites comes from the paralysis tick, which thankfully doesn't cause paralysis in humans – although it's a whole other story for our furry little friends. Please, please make sure to protect your pets from *In Australia there are around 70 types of tick.* ticks, people – cats and dogs may be too pure for this world, but that doesn't mean they deserve to be taken out by a tick.

Unless you're allergic, the common tick bite isn't going to cause you too much harm. However, there are a few unpleasant symptoms; the first and most obvious of these is the tiny bug that's lodged itself inside you. Other symptoms include:

* Rashes
* Headache
* Fever
* Flu-like symptoms
* Sore glands

✳ **Itching** at the site of the bite
✳ **A paralysed** face

If you're allergic, the symptoms can be more extreme, including:

✳ **Swollen** throat
✳ **Difficulty** breathing
✳ **Fainting**

If you experience any of this, you should seek medical attention immediately. You can kill the tick, but don't try to remove it yourself. If you're not allergic, do the following.

✳ **Do not squeeze** the tick – this will force it to squirt its icky bug juices into you, which can make the symptoms worse.
✳ **Kill the tick** – this can be done with a product containing ether (like Elastoplast Cold Spray or Wart-Off Freeze) or tea-tree oil.
✳ **Use a pair** of fine-tipped forceps (these need to be smaller than average household tweezers) and grab the tick as close to the skin as possible.

BASIC
WISDOM
FROM AN
ENGINEER

A WISE ENGINEER once told me that the difference between electrical and mechanical is that mechanical is moving parts, while electrical is moving electrons. Unfortunately, there are many moments in life where we will have to attempt to fix things using tools we don't understand while attempting not to electrocute ourselves. This wise engineer has more practical know-how in one finger than I have in my entire body, so it was only natural to approach him for the answers to those heinous and practical questions I have been avoiding the answers to for the entirety of my adult life.

CHANGING WHEELS IS TYRE-SOME

Knowing how to change a tyre feels like something that should come automatically with car ownership. At this point in our sad, adult existences, it's clear that nothing in life comes easily, and we have to learn how to do a lot of stupid tasks that will probably only be necessary once in our short and burdensome lives. Luckily, mechanical engineers are far superior to us commonfolk in all things car related, and are often willing to provide instructions to lesser humans on how to maintain their vehicles.

ASSESS YOUR TYRE

Is it actually flat, or are you just an idiot? Here are a few ways to tell:

* **You drove over** a big pothole.
* **You've pissed someone off** and they've taken revenge in the form of vehicular homicide.
* **Your car has a mind of its own** and is pulling to one side as you drive.
* **Your car is bumpy** as you drive, and you're pretty certain you haven't run anything over.
* **Your tyre looks weird** and deflated.

If you answered yes to one or more of these questions, your tyre is most likely flat – verdict still out on whether or not you're an idiot. Check your spare tyre. Is this one flat too? If so, you're fucked and should give up and call the NRMA. If your spare looks good, you may proceed.

Each car comes equipped with a jack, tyre iron and some handy tools to assist you in your emergency car repairs. These tools are usually found in the boot of your car, in the special secret compartment where the tyre is kept.

1   **Grab the jack** and the tyre iron from said secret compartment.

2   **Approach the flat tyre** and place the jack under the car. Each car has a special 'jack point' – it's important to make sure you get your jack directly under this point.

The jack point: *When you put your hand beneath the car, you should be able to feel two little grooves. This is the jack point. These grooves are generally made from two folded-over sections of metal, making them a stronger point than the rest of the car's underbelly. If you're struggling to find the jack point by hand, there should also be a guide in your car manual.*

Shit you should know

3   **Once you're sure** you've found the jack point and placed the jack beneath it, use the tyre iron to wind the jack until it comes into contact with the point. The jack needs to be perfectly aligned with the jack point – cars are heavy and if you try to lift it from another place, you will crack and damage the underside of your car. NEVER attempt to change a tyre on uneven ground – your car will be unbalanced and likely to topple off the jack.

4   **Wind the jack** until it's tight beneath the car; the jack should be supporting the car until the wheel is hovering slightly off the ground. This is as close as

you're ever going to get to owning a hover car, so enjoy it while you can.

5   **Use the tyre iron** to loosen the bolts (lefty loosey, righty tighty!). These bolts will be very tight because mechanics use a rattle gun to fix them during your service, and unfortunately, you are a puny human. As such, you'll have to use a bit of elbow grease to release these bolts. Hook the tyre iron to the bolt, then, while holding the furthest end of the tyre iron, use your body weight to release the bolt. At this point, you just want to crack the bolts open, not remove them entirely!

6   **Jack the tyre** all the way off the ground.

7   **Completely remove** the remaining bolts by hand. This goes without saying, but don't lose the bolts; you're going to need these later.

8   **Remove the tyre** from the frame and place underneath the car – this is a safety precaution so if your jack breaks and drops the car, the tyre will provide a little padding and prevent extra damage. You'll still be fucked, but slightly less fucked than you would have been, and that should always be appreciated.

9   **Put your new tyre** on the car. For a long time, I called the place where the bolts sit the 'bolt-holes', which I think we can all agree sounds hilarious and just a little dirty. The wise engineer has informed me that these are actually called the 'wheel studs', which is obviously not as good as bolt-hole, but still sort of dirty, so I'll allow it.

10 **Place the bolts** on the wheel studs and tighten them as much as you can with your fingers. You want to place the bolts on in alternate corners so the tyre ends up flat on the wheel hub – if you start all on one side and work your way around, you'll end up with a skewed wheel.

11 **Use the jack** to lower the wheel to the ground until it's hovering about a centimetre above the road.

12 **Finish tightening** the bolts with the tyre iron.

13 **Release the jack** entirely and appreciate your handy work. You just did a thing!

The word 'jack' has now lost all meaning to me, but the sacrifice is worth it since you now have one more adult skill to add to your repertoire.

CAR CPR: JUMPSTARTING A CAR

You're ready for the day. Dressed like a professional, shoes on, you walk outside and take in the world. Nothing can stop you! You get in your car, perfect driving playlist ready to blast through your aux cable, and place your keys in the ignition. But instead of the full-throttle sound of your engine waking up, you're met with a series of sad, defeated clicking noises.

Fortunately, unlike changing a tyre, jumpstarting a car is a relatively simple process. Unfortunately, jumpstarting a car is an activity that requires more tools than are supplied in the standard car toolbox. To jumpstart your car, you'll need a set of jumper cables, so having a pair of these tucked away in your car at all times will promote you to official 'Prepared Adult' status, and is therefore a worthwhile purchase for the prestige alone.

Your battery is flat, and your life may as well be over.

Aside from jumper cables, you'll also need a working car. When your battery dies in a suburban street, this ingredient is easy to come by. When you're flat in the middle of the highway after turning off your car to have a roadside tinkle, things get a little more hairy…

If you're in possession of your two main jumpstarting requirements, you're ready to defibrillate your car!

1   **Position your working car** in front of the dead one. You want the cars to be facing each other, and close

enough for the cables to reach and not be taut. Do not let the cars touch.

2   **Make sure** the handbrakes are engaged and the ignition is turned off in both cars, then pop the hoods.

3   **Connect one end** of the positive (red) jumper cable to the dead battery. Then connect the other end to the good battery.

4   **Connect the negative** (black) jumper cable to the good battery, but DO NOT connect the other end to the negative terminal on the dead battery. Instead, clamp it to a clean, unpainted metal part of the engine of the dead car (like a bolt).

Shit you should know

Positive cables and charges on the battery will be red, and negative will be black. If for some reason the colour isn't apparent on your battery, the negative side will be the one that has a lead connecting to the body of the car.

---

5   **Turn on the engine** of the car with the good battery and let it charge the dead battery for a few minutes.

6   **Try to start your car.** If it won't start, let it continue charging for another 5 minutes. If it still doesn't start, just like you, your battery is probably beyond help.

7   **If your car does start**, remove the cables in reverse order. Leave your engine running and drive around for at least 15–20 minutes – you want your battery to have a chance to recharge.

CARS NEED LOVE TOO

There are general guidelines for when your car should be serviced, but the best person to tell you when this should happen is your mechanic or dealer (not that dealer, you fucken druggo). That handy little sticker your mechanic gives you after each service is not just for show – read its infinite wisdom.

If you've long surpassed the date on the all-knowing sticker, and are too afraid to go into the mechanic and be yelled at for your sub-par car ownership and organisational skills, there's a general timeline for how long to wait between services.

* **Minor service** every 2500 km
* **Oil change** every 10,000 km
* **Major service** every 50,000 km

In addition to servicing your car, there are a couple of other tasks that should be undertaken semi-regularly.

CHECKING YOUR TYRE PRESSURE

Your tyre pressure should be checked every month, and is something that can be done at any petrol station. It's a relatively important task, as tyres that are inflated to their correct pressure rating perform better and give you more control over your car. This also helps with your overall fuel economy and, as we've already established, you're probably poor as fuck and petrol is pricey, so every cent counts.

1   **Check the guide** on the inside of your driver-side door to see what pressure your tyres should be sitting at. Every car has a different pressure setting that accounts

for the weight of the vehicle, size of the tyres and any other car-related variables that I am thankfully not wise enough to know about.

2   **At the petrol station** pressure pump, reset the pressure value to your recommended setting using the aforementioned guide.

3   **On your tyre,** remove the cap from the little valve located on the inside rim of the wheel. Slip the pressure hose on over the valve like the proverbial condom on a banana, and release the clasp so it attaches to your tyre. The pump will automatically fill your tyre to the level you preset and make a hissing noise to let you know when it's done. Remove the hose and replace the cap. Repeat on your remaining tyres.

JUST BECAUSE YOU'RE A DIPSTICK DOESN'T MEAN YOU SHOULDN'T CHECK IT

Checking your dipstick is an easy way to assess your oil levels without taking your car to a mechanic. Oil is to a car what alcohol is to me at social events: it reduces friction and keeps everything running smoothly. Like checking your tyre pressure, it's something that should be done once a month.

1   **Your dipstick is located** under the hood of your car. In most cars, a dipstick will be red, orange or yellow, and look like a little handle. The stick is usually located towards the front of the car on the passenger side. If you can't find it by looking, check your owner's manual.

2   **Slowly pull the dipstick out** and wipe the tip on a clean piece of paper towel. This may sound dirty, but it's an important skill, so get your mind out of the fucking gutter.

3   **If the oil is chunky,** smelly, black or dark, this is a sign it needs to be changed.

4   **Dry off the dipstick** completely and insert it back into the hole (if you're reading this and thinking about anything other than an important tip for vehicle maintenance, then you need Jesus). Pull it back out immediately. This will give you a reading of how much oil you have.

5   **There are two dots** on a dipstick marking the maximum and minimum lines. The line should be halfway between these points; anything lower and you're in need of a top-up.

The older your car, the more important it is to have it serviced regularly. If you have a new car you actually give a fuck about, you should try to have it serviced as often as advised, but let's face it: cars are expensive, and laziness is key to a stress-free life.

PETROL TANKS:
FINDING THE HOLE

There is no awkwardness in life quite like that of getting to the petrol station to fill up your car and realising you've parked on the wrong side of the bowser (that's a fancy word for where the petrol lives; look at you, learning things). The fortunate few among us who have tiny cars can stretch the petrol pump all the way across, if they try real, real hard. But for the rest of us, this horrendous situation means doing the reverse-out-and-reposition manoeuvre under the judgey and disdainful glares of petrol patrons and store clerks alike.

It turns out there's been a means to avoid this awkwardness all along. In every car there's a dashboard, and in that dashboard there's a fuel display. In newer cars, this fuel display has a little image of a fuel pump with a tiny arrow pointing left or right. This arrow is pointing to the side where your fuel cap is, and you are so very welcome.

If you're driving an older car, you may just have an image of a fuel pump sans arrow. Never fear! The side that the nozzle is placed on in this image is the side the fuel goes in. Again, you're welcome. Now your only excuse for terrible petrol-related awkwardness is your own stupidity.

Shit you should know

We can all agree that the physical activity and awkward conversation involved in filling up your car are the worst aspects of vehicle ownership. But did you know, most cars have between 48–183 km left in the tank after they hit empty? That range is totally dependant on the make and year of your car, not to mention how well you look after it, but who cares about those things?

WHAT IS A FUSE BOX AND WHY DO I CARE?

Electricity. What is it? How does it work? How likely am I to electrocute myself while making toast? What I can tell you is that if you live in a house, your house has a house for its electricity, and that house is a fuse box. Are you with me? Probably not, but I'm going to keep going with this metaphor, anyway. Every house has a little metal box somewhere (often outside) that holds a whole bunch of switches and shit. These boxes can also be called 'circuit breakers' and are a facet of your house you shouldn't need to interact with on the reg, but knowing their location will make it seem like you have at least some control over your life.

> Your fuse box distributes power through your home and is generally something you shouldn't fuck with.

Your interaction with the fuse box should be as minimal as your contact with that weird cousin you only see at family functions: fleeting and avoided whenever possible.

However, power outages are one rare instance in which you will have to engage with your fuse box. Some power outages are caused by blown fuses, usually the result of faulty light bulbs, old wiring, or too many appliances being used on one circuit. These things can trip a fuse and cause the power to go out. For example, if you were microwaving popcorn while boiling the kettle and making toast, you fucked up and a journey to the fuse box is the only solution.

Once you've located your fuse box, make sure all of the switches are facing the same direction. If you've blown a fuse, there'll be one switch dancing to the beat of its own drum and pointing in a different direction to the rest. Flip this switch to the right direction as you cry, 'LET THERE BE LIGHT!'

It goes without saying (but I'm going to say it anyway as I don't want to be held accountable for you electrocuting yourself) that if your fuse box is sparking, dripping with water, on fire, or doing anything other than being a stationary box filled with switches, don't fucking touch it. Light a candle, make your popcorn on the stove like they did in the olden days, and call an electrician.

SPANNERS, SCREWDRIVERS AND OTHER HANDY TOOLS

Living out of home means there are a few things worth investing in: your own set of towels, a washing basket, a first-aid kit that contains more than just Panadol and band-aids, and a basic toolbox. If you're anywhere near as hopeless as I am, the toolbox and first-aid kit should be kept within close proximity of each other.

Whether your toolbox is an old plastic bag or a tattered cardboard box, every wannabe adult should be in possession of the following implements:

* **Tape measure.**
* **Torch** – because sometimes you have to fix things in the dark.
* **Level** – sometimes adults hang pictures on their walls. A great way to assess someone's adult capabilities is whether or not said pictures are straight or crooked.
* **Electric drill.**
* **Extension cord.**
* **Ladder.**
* **Shovel** – you never know when you'll want to pretend you're good at gardening.
* **Hacksaw** – we all know your life is a horror film, so you definitely want one of these lying around for your potential murderer to kill you with.
* **Hammer** – preferably one with a claw; not only are they good for banging shit in, they're also great for pulling it back out again when you realise you've put it in the wrong place.
* **Stanley knife** – very fun, but very sharp. Keep away

from children, aka you (you're reading a book called *How to Adult*; you should not be in charge of anything with a sharp edge).

* **Spanner** – the U-shaped tool used on bolts. Your secret in-car toolbox probably has one of these, so feel free to ransack before investing in one of your own.

* **Screwdriver** – there are two different types of screwdrivers: flat-head and Phillips. While flat-head is fairly self-explanatory, Phillip was obviously named after some self-obsessed tool who loved screwing around.

And there you have it: a full list of all the adult fix-it utensils you should have (but definitely don't). Now go on an excursion to Bunnings and start a collection that all suburban fathers will be jealous of for years to come.

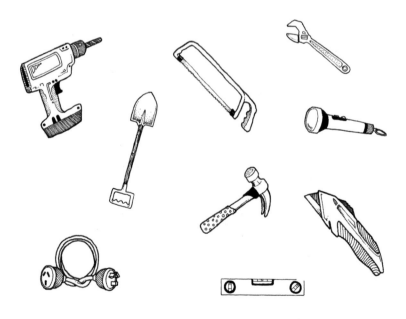

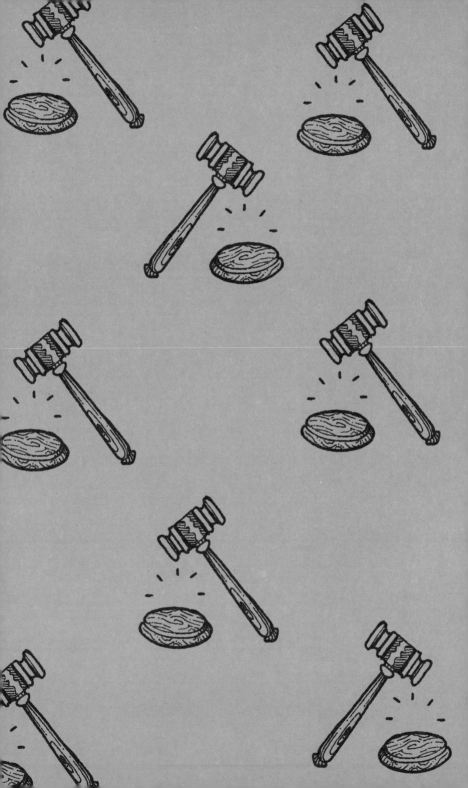

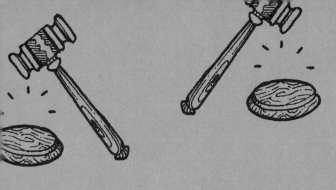

LEGAL ADVICE
FOR WHEN YOU'RE
TOO POOR
FOR A
LAWYER

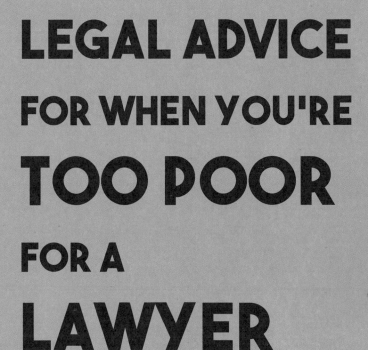

THE LAW. It's big, it's scary, it's confusing as fuck. Have you broken it without knowing? Probably. Are you living a life of crime and sin, constantly fearing apprehension? Most definitely. Luckily, my utter lack of knowledge regarding all things law led me to a wise adult who has more life experience and expertise than I can ever comprehend, let alone hope to achieve. This informed lawyer taught me all the things my foolish millennial mind struggled to grasp, and answered the burning legal questions that have been bothering me for the last two and a half decades. Feast your eyes on his wisdom and try to move past your life of crime.

WILL YOURSELF TO DEATH:
DO YOU NEED A WILL?

Here's the deal: realistically, you're only ever going to need a will if you've popped out a kid or two who will need to be looked after in the event of your untimely demise, or you're in possession of assets worth distributing to your loved ones (or enemies, depending on what brand of fucked-up human you are/how much haunting you plan on doing); although, this book is in your possession and it's probably one of the most valuable things you've ever owned.

> Give your loved ones a
> post—death power ranking by
> leaving them behind your most
> prized possession, or a pair of
> unwashed socks.

There are a few things to keep in mind if you are, in fact, adult enough to have assets that require divvying up once you cark it.

* **If you have a will** and then get married, your previous will is no longer valid. So, when you're preparing yourself to be shackled down, add 'update my will' to that long and scary to-do list of adult responsibilities. Fun fact: this rule doesn't apply to de-facto relationships, but they do have other rights regarding possessions and death of a partner – but more on that happy topic later!

* **If you don't have a will**, then your assets will be distributed based on a formula. This formula is determined on a state-by-state basis. Generally, your money (including savings and super) will go to your

next of kin or partner. However, this is not always the case, and if you want to be 100% sure your money will go to who you want it to (even if it's only $5 worth of silver coins in the bottom of your handbag), you need to have a will that clearly outlines where and how you want your money distributed.

✳ **Even after you die**, your body still hangs around causing trouble. One of the beauties of having a will is that you can stipulate exactly what you want to happen with your manky corpse. When you make a will, you assign an 'executor' – anyone over 18 who is capable of ensuring your wishes are followed. Despite wills giving you the opportunity to specify what you want done with your body, this isn't as binding as what happens to your possessions, the reason being that people are fucking crazy and often have completely ridiculous wishes for their burial rites. So, if you want your ashes to be blasted out of a bazooka over an unsuspecting crowd of people, make sure you pick someone fucking cool as your executor who will be sure to carry out your final wishes.

Shit you should know

Just because you have a will, doesn't mean that when you die people automatically know what will happen with all your shit. You need to store your will somewhere people will be able to find it once you die and let another living person know where it is. If you both die in the same tragic accident, then you're pretty much fucked.

BUT WHAT ABOUT MY NAPKIN WILL?

When I was 16, I realised I had quite a sizeable collection of books and CDs that I didn't want going to my younger brother after my death (at that point, I was fairly certain he would be the cause of my imminent demise, but that's all speculation). So, every year after my birthday I would write an unofficial will and hide it in my room for my parents to find, just in case. Up until I conducted the interviews for this book, I still believed this was a completely foolproof and enlightened method of protecting my assets. As it turns out, a will written by an underaged lunatic on a scrap of paper is not actually an official document, and legal wills require some legal proceedings in order to be valid.

* **Your will must be in writing,** either typed or handwritten.
* **Your will needs to be signed** by you (the will-maker). If you're in no capacity to sign your will then a representative can sign it on your behalf.
* **Your signature needs to be witnessed** by at least two people at the same time. Both of these witnesses must be independent from the will and not beneficiaries.
* **Your signature** (or your designated signer's signature) must be made with the intention of executing the will in the future.

> *Witnesses to wills have to physically be able to see you sign the will. This means that anyone who is blind or vision impaired – temporarily or otherwise – is not eligible to witness a will.*
>
> Shit you should know

While there are a few things you need for a will to be official, there's a relatively short list of things that are not 100% necessary:

* **You don't need to sign the will at the foot** of the document. I know, I know, that's how they do it in all the movies, but as is so often the case, the movies lie!
* **Your witness does not need** to know that it's your will they're witnessing; you could tell them you're signing an NDA for some crazy spy shit or something – it doesn't matter. Be like the movies and lie away!

I HAD AN ACCIDENT, NOW WHAT?

The glaringly obvious first step if you're in a car accident is to assess whether you, your passengers or any of the people in the other car (or cars) are injured. In the unfortunate event that someone is injured, make sure there are no hazards around (like your car is on fire, or other cars on the road), then call 000. As we've already established, there are about a billion people in this world who are more qualified than you at many things. Unless you yourself are an EMT, first aid and emergency response are two things that you are not qualified to do. Additionally, if there are any injuries incurred from the accident, you're obligated to call the police. If no one is injured and your car is blocking traffic, take photos of the scene and move your car. If it's not possible to move your car, turn the hazard lights on.

Once you've assessed whether anyone is injured, and the amount of damage caused by your accident, there's a checklist of things you should go through:

* **Are you insured?** You should probably know the answer to this one before you get in an accident…
* **Collect the details** of the other party. You need to know:
    - Whether they are insured. If so, who with?
    - Their name, phone number, address and a photo of their driver's licence.
    - The details of their car: registration number, colour, make and model.
* **Take photos** of the damage, and be as thorough as possible.

WHAT DE FUCKTO?

Story time: when I was in my early twenties, I had been living with my boyfriend for two and a half years. We were both enjoying the young and carefree life of living out of home as pretend adults with part-time jobs and half-finished university degrees. One day, I was speaking to an older relative when he made a joke about my de-facto relationship status. His joke turned out to be not all that funny, and I was given the unpleasant and disgustingly adult realisation that for the last six months I had essentially been married to my partner. Suffice to say, this was far too adult for both of us, and we immediately had to do everything in our power to downgrade our new and horrific adult status, namely playing a lot of video games, drinking in excess and eating enough pizza to put us both in early graves.

Alert your side hoes: turns out you can be in a de facto with more than one partner at a time. Although de facto is a relationship defined as being between two people, you can be in multiple de factos at one time – not to mention a de-facto relationship can also exist when one partner is married to someone else. It's every polygamist's dream!

Shit you should know

For those of you who haven't upsettingly been found in the middle of an accidental de-facto relationship, they are actually a great alternate (or prequel) to marriage – especially prior to the legalisation of same-sex marriage in Australia. Being in a de-facto relationship gives you similar rights to a married couple, and although not exactly the same (de-facto relationships are still a lot more fluid and undefined than marriages), de factos are an important aspect of protecting your rights within a relationship.

There are only three requirements for the legal definition of a de-facto relationship:

1   **You are not legally married** to each other (that would be called a marriage, duh).

2   **You are not related** by family (this one is called incest, folks).

3   **Your relationship** is that of a couple living on a 'genuine domestic basis'.

The definition of a de-facto relationship really comes down to the vague statement: *genuine domestic partnership*. While there are a set of factors to determine how genuine your domestic partnership is, there's no rule as to how many of these need to be fulfilled for you to classify as being de facto. If you did need to go to court and prove your relationship, each of the following factors would be subject to a jury and it would be their verdict that ultimately determined the validity of your relationship.

* **The duration** of your relationship; two years is the generally accepted timeline, but there are exceptions to this, namely if you have kids together.
* **Your living arrangements** (e.g. do you live together? Do you share a bedroom in your shared home?).
* **How your finances** are arranged and how financially dependent you are on each other.
* **Whether a sexual relationship** exists (have fun chatting about that one with the courts).
* **The way you present** your relationship in public (e.g. is your relationship status up on Facebook? When

was the last time you shared a photo together? Social media is the key to a legit relationship, obviously).

✳ **The degree** of commitment to a shared life.

✳ **Whether you own property** together, and how you bought that property.

✳ **Whether your relationship is registered** with the state. Registering your relationship isn't required for a de-facto relationship – however, if you're desperate for your relationship to be acknowledged, but won't (or can't) get married, then this is the way to do it.

✳ **Whether you have** or care for children together.

All these factors are great in providing a general guideline as to what is and isn't classified as a de-facto relationship, but the most commonly accepted definition is two people who have been living together in a 'marriage-like' way for at least two years. All those other rules really only come into play if you're in a situation in which you want to prove (or deny…) your relationship status.

'TIL DEATH DO US PART

As with any other relationship, sometimes de factos can kick the bucket. In the case of a break-up or a partner dying, the rules and rights for people in de factos are pretty similar to that of those in marriages.

A separation agreement is the simplest way to ensure you're protected in the result of a de facto break-up. Like a prenup, there's a certain amount of stigma around these worst-case scenario documents. While I'm a millennial who avoids preparing for the future by all means possible, I'm also a cynic with an unending belief that all good things must come to an end – and in general, people are pretty shit.

In a more morbid turn of events, if your de-facto partner happens to die and hasn't accounted for you in their will, you can contest this on the basis of your relationship status. This is the time for that handy genuine-domestic-partnership checklist to shine! And if your de-facto partner wasn't living by my 'hope for the best but prepare for the worst' mentality and didn't have a will prepared at all, as long as you live at least 30 days after their death, you become entitled to their estate.

A separation agreement helps to reduce uncertainty around splitting assets, who pays previously shared bills, or who looks after any kids in the event of a nasty break-up.

To add another element to the mix, if your partner didn't have a will but *did* have children from a previous relationship, they too can be entitled to the estate. These are the situations in which it's best to consult a lawyer, because we both know this book is not the answer to that mammoth problem.

HOLLA, 'WE WANT PRENUP!'

Marriage: it's a big scary lifelong commitment. Except 48.3% of the time it's not… The average marriage in Australia lasts about 12 years, which seems to be the global average, with the US and France sitting at around 13 years, and Japan, Russia and the UK sticking it out for 11. That's just enough time to have some cool shit to your name, only to have it ripped away from you in a trashy and bitter divorce. This is where prenuptial agreements come in. You're better off having one because, in the words of Kanye West, 'When she leave yo' ass, she gon' leave with half.'

Like wills, prenups require a little more effort than a handwritten document drawn up on a napkin.

A prenup is also referred to as a 'binding financial agreement'. Put simply, it's an agreement settled on by two people to record their assets and decide what will happen to those assets if the relationship ends. For a prenup to be considered a valid legal document, it must fulfil the following criteria.

* **It must comply** with the legal guidelines of the *Family Law Act 1975*.
* **It must be in writing** – a verbal agreement that you guys will evenly divide your shitty kitchen utensils is not going to hold up in court.
* **Each party must receive** independent legal advice on the contract.
* **Said legal advice** needs to be provided by a lawyer from the Australian jurisdiction.
* **A prenup must be signed voluntarily,** meaning

you can't coerce your future spouse into signing the document by telling them you won't marry them if they don't; not only is this illegal, but it also makes you a bit of a dick…

✳ **The prenup needs to contain** a completely honest disclosure of the assets of each party.

When it comes to hoping for the best and preparing for the worst, prenups are the ultimate solution. Love is great and everything, but given the astronomically high divorce rate that only seems to be rising each year, it makes sense to protect yourself and your partner from any unnecessary nastiness post-divorce. In fact, it's a well-accepted fact that having a prenup actually strengthens a relationship; there can be no doubt that your partner is marrying you for you and not your money. Really, if you ain't no punk, holla 'We want prenup!'

I DON'T WANT TO LIVE IN THIS COUNTRY ANYMORE

Despite the glory of this sunburnt country and 'land of sweeping plains', there may come a time when you can no longer stomach the musical-chairs political system, overwhelming statistics of violence against women, and deep-seated alcohol issues our country is so well known for, and are forced to go in search of greener pastures.

In the event you do choose to move overseas in search of a country that doesn't ignore its Indigenous history and has a refugee policy that's less fucked up than ours, there are some organisational details that should be accounted for.

* **Visas:** If you're planning on getting a job overseas or staying for any extended period of time, it's almost certain you're going to need some form of visa. The best way to assess what kind of visa you need is through the embassy of your chosen country. Note that every visa is different, and countries have different regulations around how visas are renewed and applied for. Be 100% sure you completely understand the stipulations of your visa, and don't be like my cousin who was detained in the Ukraine for a week because she overstayed her visa in Italy. Being alone and held in a country where you don't speak the language is probably at the bottom of your list of things to do abroad.

* **Tax:** As we've established, tax is one of those dreaded and unavoidable aspects of adult existence and, seriously, can it just not? Unfortunately, the only release from the scourge of taxes is death, so even escaping the country won't save you. When you move overseas, there

are a number of tax-related questions to ask yourself.
- Where will you be a resident?
- Is this a permanent or temporary move?
- Where is the most advantageous place for you to be paying tax?

All these questions are dependent on which country you are moving to, your income, whether or not you have a HECS debt, and what type of visa you're on. Before you move overseas for an extended period of time, it's definitely worth visiting an accountant to find out how to best manage your new taxation situation and make sure you get the best deal – paying double tax is not something anyone wants to do.

＊ **Savings:** If you're in any way prepared to move overseas, you probably have a sweet little nest egg of savings to cushion the transition to your new home. If you're planning on moving away for a long period of time, maybe even forever, you'll probably want to consider getting a bank account in your new country of residence, and maybe converting your money to the currency of your new location. Keep in mind, changing from one currency to another can be risky. If the exchange rate changes dramatically (or even slightly, depending on the sum of money you've converted), then you could lose out on a whole bunch of your hard-earned cash.

＊ **Health:** Did you know that not all countries are the same? There are so many varied ecosystems and habitats across the globe, which means that moving overseas will expose you to entirely new foods, animals, people, germs, infections, illnesses, causes of death, and all the fun things! If you're moving somewhere you know has a vastly different ecosystem, it's advisable to visit your doctor and see if there are any shots or vaccinations you may need before entering the country. The same goes for general overseas travel – no one wants their first global tour to be ruined by rabies. It's also worth noting that access to healthcare differs greatly from country to country.

* **Renting:** If you plan to rent overseas, find out what the terms of rental contracts are before you leave. Some countries require a local guarantor for all rental agreements, and if you're alone in a new country, or only know other emigrants, then you're going to be living in a hostel for the foreseeable future.

* **Mail:** You're probably not important enough to be receiving anything other than Woolies brochures and parking fines in the mail, but if you don't want your parents to be spammed with your depressing post, it's worth investing in a PO box or having your letters redirected elsewhere before you move away.

* **Voting:** Sometimes we have elections, and despite our government's apparent inability to listen to the people, your opinion is still required. If you've moved overseas, you can vote online in local, state and federal elections. The Australian Electoral Committee has an entire webpage filled with forms for overseas Australians who wish to vote. They also have a mailing list that will inform you of any upcoming elections to ensure you don't miss out on your civic duty. Oh joy!

* **Laws:** Although there are some laws that stay relatively the same no matter where you are, it's pretty safe to assume that every country will have a few different aspects to their legal systems. If you plan on breaking any laws overseas, make sure you know what the repercussions are – something that incurs a minor punishment in Australia could have far more severe repurcussions overseas.

A lot of the necessary documentation and preparation for moving abroad is dependent on where you're going, so the biggest take-home message here is: do your research!

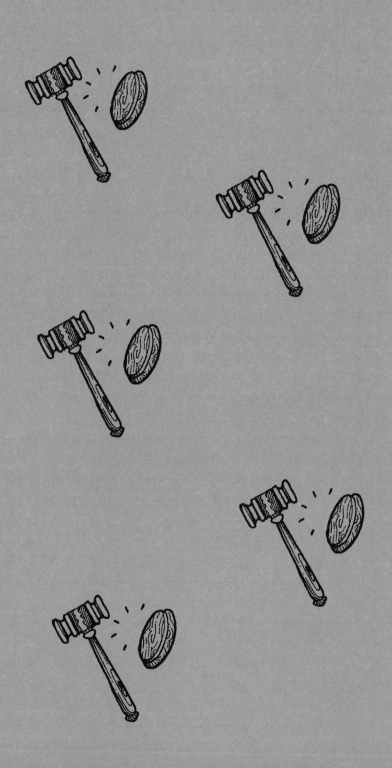

JARGON AROUND

Of all the impressive adult jobs, being a lawyer is right up there with accountants, doctors and astronauts. And while few of us are diligent and boring enough to commit to the extensive study required to actually become a lawyer, the rest of us can simply spruce up our vocabularies with a shit-ton of fancy lawyer words that will make us seem like high-functioning academics who know what's really going on.

* **Jurisdiction:** the extent of legal authority or power of the court to apply the law.
* **Mediation:** the process in which a third party assists in bringing about a settlement or compromise to avoid taking a matter to court.
* **Affidavit:** a written statement provided by a party or witness.
* **Appeal:** a procedure where a decision made by the court can be challenged.
* **Barrister:** a lawyer who specialises in court work.
* **Injunction:** a court order that asks someone to do (or stop doing) something.
* **Litigation:** a court dispute; a lawsuit.
* **Subpoena:** a summons ordering a witness or agency to attend court or offer evidence.
* **Adjourn:** to suspend a court hearing.
* **Annuity:** a yearly payable sum of money.
* **Beneficiary:** someone who is left something in a will.
* **Codicil:** a document signed by a will-maker that adds or alters a pre-existing will.
* **Defamation:** to say derogatory statements about another person with no justification.
* **Duress:** to place pressure on a person in order to force them to do or say something.

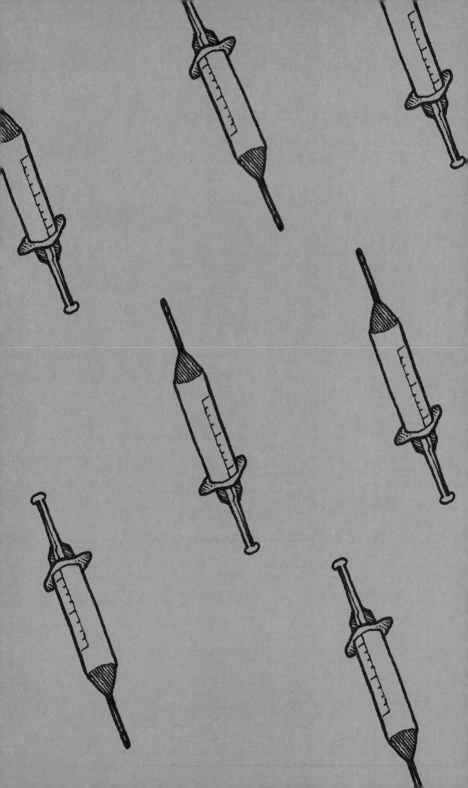

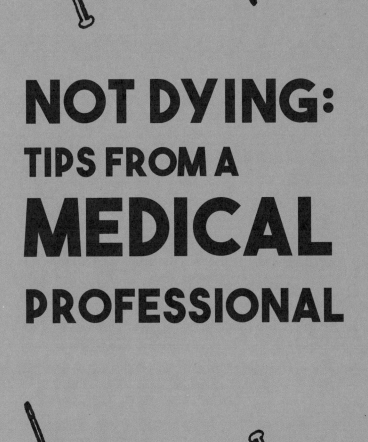

NOT DYING:
TIPS FROM A
MEDICAL
PROFESSIONAL

BEFORE I REACHED peak adulthood, I believed that the truest sign of my maturity would be when I stopped injuring myself frequently and foolishly. Unfortunately for my bruised and battered body, it turns out getting older is not a cure for clumsiness or bad decision-making. In fact, it seems as if ridiculous and avoidable injuries have become more frequent, and the only thing that's changed has been my capacity to deal with them myself, rather than consulting my mother for each one. On the plus side, she's now far less privy to how much of a mess I am... at least until she reads this book.

There's no doubt in anyone's mind that my knowledge of all things adult is second to none, but I'm still waiting on that honorary doctorate I can show off at parties and use to earn the respect of the medical community and world at large. While you'll be tempted to take my word as gospel, there's only so much this book can do to rescue you from the burns, suspect itches and near-death experiences of adult life. So despite the fact that I'm hooked up with some sick medical connections, and had no shame in asking them to fix my – and to a further extent, your – life problems, medical advice is best sought from a professional who can fully assess the disgusting inner workings of your body.

WHAT'S IN THE BOX?

As it turns out, first-aid kits are better for more than just loose band-aids and that delicious purple cough syrup your parents spoonfed you as a child. Real grown-ups keep their first-aid kits in cool, dry places, and stock them with an assortment of important medical things, including, but not limited to:

* **Bandages**, plasters and sterile gauze dressings in various sizes
* **Safety pins**
* **Disposable gloves** (the sterile kind)
* **Scissors**
* **Antiseptic cleaning wipes** and antiseptic cream
* **Thermometer** (preferably digital – you're not smart or hipster enough for the analogue version)
* **Rash creams**, such as hydrocortisone
* **Treatments** for bites or stings, like Stingose or SOOV
* **Painkillers**, like paracetamol, aspirin or ibuprofen
* **Cough medicine** (the yummy purple stuff, for nostalgia)
* **Antihistamine** tablets

DO I NEED TO GO TO THE HOSPITAL?

There's a time in every adult's life where you fuck up so badly that you are forced to ask the question, 'Do I need to go to the hospital for this?'

In my vast experience, most of these situations are coupled with excessive drinking and friends as ill-equipped to handle the situation as you are. When in doubt, there's only one solution: let someone else decide for you!

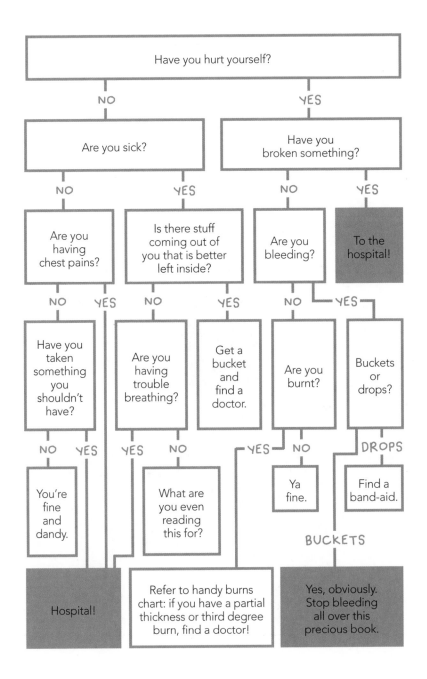

SICK BURN: FROM INSULTS TO SUNBURN

Skin is more than one big fleshy person-suit that you wear like a glove. As it turns out, skin is the largest organ of the human body, and is made up of three layers:

* **The epidermis:** This is the top layer of the skin, and the barrier between our insidey parts and the outside world. The epidermis protects your precious gooey innards from infection and environmental pathogens.

* **The dermis:** The main section of the skin. This middle layer contains all the good shit; our blood and lymph vessels, hair follicles and glands all hang out in this fleshy patch. The dermis also does a whole bunch of other neat things, like housing the glands that produce sweat and regulate our body temperature, as well as producing sebum, an oily goop that keeps our skin moist. The dermis is basically the powerhouse of the skin, and way more relevant and important than you will ever be.

* **The hypodermis:** Also called the subcutaneous tissue, this is the third and final layer of the skin. It's mainly made up of loose connective tissue and fat, not to mention some large blood vessels and nerves. In short, this is the layer of skin that you never, ever want to be able to see. Keep that shit all up inside ya where it belongs.

Now that we know that the skin is more than just a fleshy organ sack, we can start to understand the varying degrees of burns and how to measure their severity.

SUPERFICIAL BURNS: ooh, that smarts

Also known as first-degree burns, these are the burns that you, as a hopeless adult, will probably encounter often. A superficial burn is one that occurs on your epidermis. First-degree burns are generally caused by sunburn, scalding or electric shocks, and although they are the least serious and usually won't require medical attention, there are a few things you can do to treat these burns yourself:

* **Ibuprofen or paracetamol** can both be taken to relieve some of the discomfort. Ibuprofen will likely be more useful in treating this pain because of its anti-inflammatory properties.
* **Run cool water** over the burn for a minimum of 20 minutes, then place a cool compress on the area. DO NOT USE ICE! Although it may be soothing, using ice on a burn can cause further tissue damage.
* **Once the skin has cooled**, use a moisturising ointment, like aloe vera.
* **Cover the burn** with a clean, non-stick dressing.

PARTIAL-THICKNESS BURNS: that's going to leave a mark

Commonly referred to as second-degree burns, these are burns that affect both the epidermis and the dermis and are usually caused by scalding, chemical burns or direct flames. Second-degree burns often cause pain, redness, swelling and blistering and are generally not a good time.

The treatment for second-degree burns is much the same as it is for first-degree burns, but if the blisters burst you are at a high risk of infection. With this in mind, it's important to be cautious of your blisters by treating them gently and covering them with a clean dressing. If you do burst your blisters and get an infection, visit your doctor for an antibiotic.

FULL-THICKNESS BURNS: you done fucked up

Known as third-degree burns, and generally caused by liquid scalding and extended contact with hot items or flames, these are as bad as a burn can possibly get. If you've burnt yourself this badly, you need to put this book down immediately and head straight to hospital. If you couldn't already tell, cold water and Panadol just aren't going to cut it. Wrap the burn in a clean, dry, cotton cloth to protect it from pressure and friction and go to the nearest hospital.

SICK BURNS

While medical treatment is often the solution to most physical ailments, we all know that Western medicine has its flaws. What big pharma doesn't want you to know is that laughter is the greatest cure of all. What could brighten a hospital room more than a barrage of insults, designed to burn you to your very core? Next time you find yourself in a hospital room with time to kill, bust out some of these nuggets of gold.

* **Is your catheter** showing, or are you just happy to see me?
* **If laughter is** the best medicine, your face must be curing the world…
* **There's no vaccination** against stupidity.
* **If people were organs**, you'd be an appendix.
* **I'd enjoy an enema** more than talking to you.
* **You so ugly** not even a plastic surgeon could fix that hot mess!
* **God, I hope you** sued the doctor who did that to you…
* **I wish I had** Alzheimer's so I could forget how ugly you are.

HEAT OR ICE?

Ice and heat are the go-to remedies for every wannabe medic on the side of a sporting field. 'Ice it' is the frustrating advice your dad will give you when you've been pestering him about your stubbed toe or developing bruise, while every complaint over a sore muscle will be met with: 'Do you have a hot water bottle?' But what do these treatments do, and when is the right time to use them?

ICE

Ice is the best immediate treatment for acute injuries. Icing minimises swelling and reduces bleeding in the tissues, as well as alleviates muscle spasms and pain. Using a cold pack is the most effective way of reducing inflammation without resorting to drugs, and is best used within the first 48 hours of an injury. So, when you twist your ankle doing a sweet kickflip or pull a muscle as you bust a move on the DF, pop an icepack on that bad boy asap and hopefully prevent some of the damage to your body. Sadly, I have no advice for how to mend your dignity...

HEAT

Where ice is perfect for acute injuries, heat is better for more chronic issues that don't come with an immediate cause, like aches and general stiffness – you know, all those horrible pains that come hurtling towards you as you make your descent into senility. Long-term and chronic pain, such as back injuries and knee pains (oh, the joys of an adult body), are usually associated with tension and tightness; something that heat is very effective in relieving.

Using ice or heat in the wrong situation is like the male nipple: pointless and a little ridiculous. If you were to ice a stiff muscle, all you'd do is increase the stiffness and pain. By the same token, if you heat a fresh injury, you're only going to increase the inflammation and make it worse.

If you're ever in doubt again, remember: ice for acute, heat for obtuse. Simple.

> If this book has taught you one thing it should be that you can never have too much knowledge! Enrolling in a first-aid course is one of the best ways to ensure you have the skills to get you out of sticky medical situations. In Australia, St John Ambulance, TAFE and the Red Cross run regular courses, all of which cover basic first aid and CPR.
>
> Shit you should know

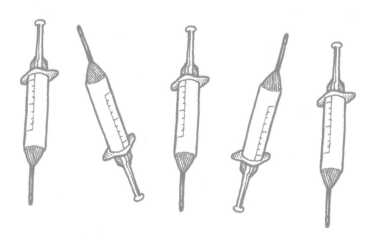

WHICH PILL SHOULD I POP?

Knowing which pain relief to use is made a lot easier when you also have a general understanding of how these drugs affect your physiology. Plus, it makes you sound hella smart when you can tell people what an analgesic is and give a definition of NSAIDs. Get learned.

Analgesic is a common word for drugs that act to relieve pain. Please note, it is pronounced AN-algesic, not anal-gesic. Don't embarrass yourself.

Shit you should know

PARACETAMOL

This is a first-line analgesic, and is most effective for mild pain and fever. Scientists aren't exactly sure how paracetamol actually works (which is very reassuring…) but their best guess is that it has an effect on the central nervous system that reduces the intensity of pain signals to the brain. Paracetamol is generally suggested to treat pains such as:

* Headaches
* Muscle pain
* Toothaches
* Arthritis
* Cold and flu symptoms
* Fever

In the correct dosage, paracetamol won't cause stomach irritation, so it's the perfect treatment for when you need pain relief but are too sick or sore to eat before taking it. That doesn't mean that taking paracetamol is without risks. If you exceed the recommended daily dose of 4 grams (8 x 500 mg tablets), you can damage your liver, and you need that to drink away your problems.

IBUPROFEN

This is a non-steroidal anti-inflammatory drug (also known as an NSAID). Ibuprofen is a second-line analgesic, which means it can be taken on top of paracetamol if paracetamol alone is not enough. Ibuprofen is used to reduce mild or moderate pain, and has anti-inflammatory benefits. It works by stopping your body from producing large amounts of prostaglandins. If, like me, you're too uneducated to know what prostaglandins are, they are hormones that are released into your body when you're injured or sick, making your nerves more sensitive to pain. These substances make tissues inflamed and swollen, and taking an ibuprofen reduces that inflammation. Ibuprofen is best for targeting pain from things like:

* Headaches
* Muscle pain
* Fever
* Cold and flu symptoms
* Period pain
* Back pain
* Dental pain
* Joint pain
* Sinus pain

Ibuprofen is not gentle on the stomach and overuse can cause stomach bleeding, which while being very metal is impractical for general life. Ibuprofen should always be taken with food, and although my motto is that everything in life is made better with the consumption of alcohol, this is one of the few exceptions.

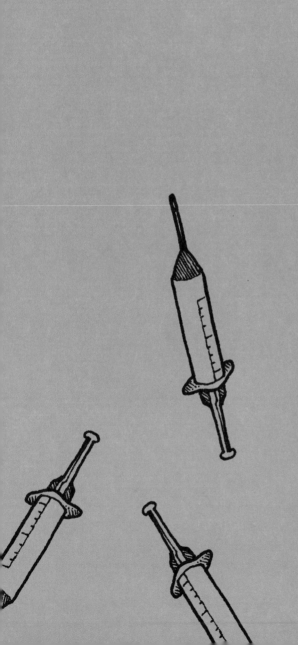

BITE ME

Nothing likes you. Everyone thinks you're trash, so much so that there's a vast array of non-humans simply dying to sink their teeth into you, ranging from the tiniest ant to the biggest shark. Sadly, if something as sizable as a shark chows down on you, there's not a whole lot this book can do for you… Small, manageable bites – now that's something I can advise on!

ANT BITES AND BEE STINGS

If you get attacked by a bee, the first step is to remove the stinger as quickly as you can to reduce the amount of venom in your system. Don't use tweezers; this will just squeeze all that bee juice right into you. Instead, scrape or brush the stinger off, using your hand.

Next, run the bite or sting under cold water. If the inflammation is really bad, you can apply an icepack – the cold will help ease itching and irritation later so you don't fuck around with the wound too much.

> *Not all bees die when they sting! The queen honey bee and bumblebees are both able to sting repeatedly. Luckily for us, queen bees don't typically venture far from the hive, and bumblebees are the chill stoners of the bee family. Nevertheless, bees have been playing us all along and definitely can't be trusted.*
>
> Shit you should know

Here's the next test of your adulting skills: using your well-stocked first-aid kit, locate your Stingose ointment or SOOV and apply it to the bite. If your discomfort continues, you can take an oral antihistamine to help with the irritation and swelling.

If you're allergic to bees or ants, things get a whole lot more dramatic. You'll likely go into anaphylactic shock. If this isn't your first allergic reaction, hopefully you'll be prepared with an EpiPen; if not call 000 IMMEDIATELY and try to stay as calm as possible while waiting for help to arrive.

SNAKE BITES

Did you know that Australia has over 140 species of land snakes and 32 species of sea snakes? It's something you can never un-know, so enjoy trying to sleep at night thinking about the hundreds of snakes that want to eat you and everything you love. While only 100 are venomous – and only 12 of those are likely to inflict a wound that could kill you – snakes are still the most terrifying thing about being an Australian. If you are existing within a waking nightmare and do happen to be nipped by a snake, the best strategy is to stay calm and act quickly.

There are two types of snake bites: dry and venomous. A dry bite is when a snake is being an angsty motherfucker and bites you without releasing venom, just because they can. Legless arseholes…

A venomous bite is exactly what it sounds like. Not only are you being bitten, but the snake is releasing its venom into the wound. Unfortunately, it's pretty hard to tell the difference between these two bites until you start experiencing symptoms, which can range from dizziness and headaches to swelling, difficulty breathing, paralysis, coma or death. So regardless of what type of bite you think you've experienced, always seek medical attention.

Shit you should know

* **Call emergency** services immediately and apply a pressure bandage to the bite.
* **Take off any jewellery** you're wearing as your limbs can swell up so much you won't be able to get it off later.
* **Starting at the site of the bite,** use a bandage (or CLEAN ripped shirt) and firmly wrap the limb up to 15 centimetres above the wound. Keep the bandaged limb still, and keep calm and stationary. Unless you're sitting in the snake's nest.
* **DO NOT WASH THE WOUND!** Washing a snake bite means washing away the venom, which in theory sounds positive, but actually means that doctors will be unable to identify the snake that's bitten you. Identifying the snake bite means the doctors will be able to quickly and effectively treat you.

I know we've all watched Bear Grylls do some cool survival shit in our lifetimes, but please, for the love of god, do not apply a tourniquet or try to suck the venom out of the wound.

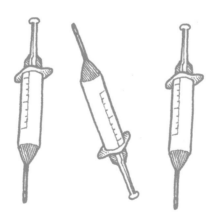

CHOKE ON THAT

We've all seen the movies where the poor, unsuspecting diner is enjoying a delicious meal when suddenly their food gets caught in their throat, they start choking, and their beautiful companion begins screaming, 'IS ANYONE HERE A DOCTOR?!'

Given you are reading this book, it seems safe to assume that you are not mentally equipped to care for yourself or others, but hopefully after consuming the wise and medically advised information in this section, you will be able to fulfil the Hollywood-hero archetype and save that restaurant patron in a blaze of glory.

Choking is generally the result of a blocked airway, and obviously the immediate solution is to clear the blockage. To do so, follow these steps.

1   **Call an ambulance!** When you dislodge the blockage, you'll want some medical professionals around to clap you on the back and congratulate you on your enormous skill.

2   **Get the choker to cough** – this might remove the blockage easily and means you can avoid human contact for another day.

3   **Give them a few blows** between the shoulder blades; make sure they're hard – this person needs to be punished for choking to begin with.

4   **If all else fails**, you can perform a chest thrust – an action that is a lot less dirty than it sounds:

- Place one hand in the middle of the choker's back for support, and to make sure you don't send them sprawling across the ground when you start beating the shit out of them.
- Place the heel of your other hand on the lower half of their sternum (that's a fancy word for breastbone for those too embarrassed to ask).
- Give them five thrusts (WITH YOUR HANDS). After each one, check to see if the blockage has been removed.
- If the victim still has a hunk of crap lodged inside them, alternate between five back blows and five chest thrusts.
- If all your blowing and thrusting is successful, the choker should be able to cough out the obstruction. If not, continue these motions in sets of five until the professional adults arrive.

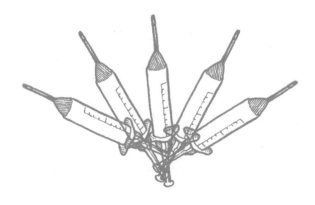

CPR: CAN'T PERFORM RAP

As mentioned at the beginning of this section, education is the key to success! The best way to learn CPR is from an expert who will be able to teach you far better than any book. That being said, it doesn't hurt to have a good idea of the basics.

1   **Before you begin CPR**, assess the situation. Is the victim in danger? Are you in danger?

2   **Call an ambulance**. Again, there are professionals who actually went to school to learn how to do this. CPR is really tiring, and you're definitely going to want someone with some experience to sub in.

3   **Interlock your hands** and give 30 chest compressions. You want to average 100–120 compressions a minute. The beat of 'Staying Alive' by the Bee Gees is the coincidentally perfect tune to pump a chest to, so have a little singalong as you save a life.

4   **Tilt the person's head back** and lift their chin to open the airway. Pinch their nostrils shut and cover their mouth with yours to make a seal.

5   **Give a breath** lasting one second and watch to see if their chest rises. If it does, give a second breath; if not, you need to re-tilt their head and try to open their airway again.

6   **Give another 30 chest compressions**, and two more breaths.

7   **Continue** this cycle until help arrives.

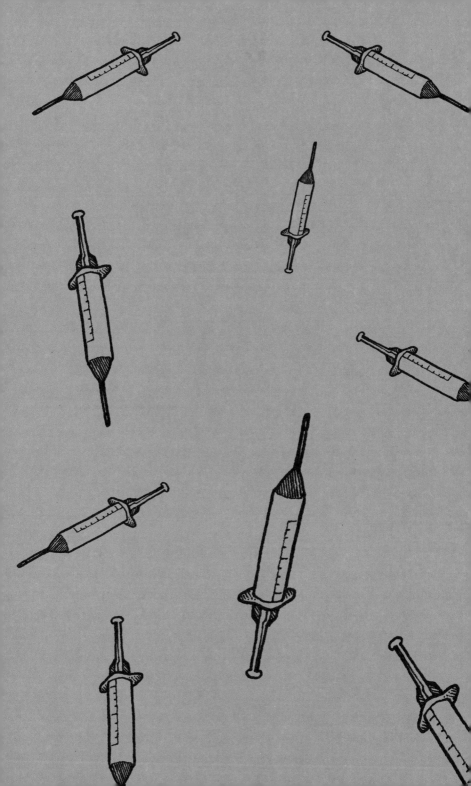

THAT'S A BIT SHOCKING:
ANAPHYLAXIS

While most of the medical issues in this section are pretty unpleasant and can be cause for a bit of drama and hysterics, anaphylactic shock is one of the biggies.

Anyone with a serious allergy knows they should always carry an EpiPen. In the event of an anaphylactic shock, this should be the first thing you use; this is a medical task basic enough that even you can perform it! Simply place the tip of the pen against the outer thigh, push in firmly until you hear a click and hold for three seconds.

Even if you manage a case of anaphylaxis, medical attention is always 100% necessary!

Other than using the EpiPen, the best thing you can do is call for help, and try to keep whoever is in shock calm.

Aside from a general fear of peanuts, some of the signs of anaphylaxis are:

* **Swelling** of the face or tongue
* **Difficulty** breathing
* **Tight feeling** in the throat
* **Hoarse voice** or difficulty speaking
* **Wheeze** or persistent cough
* **Dizziness**

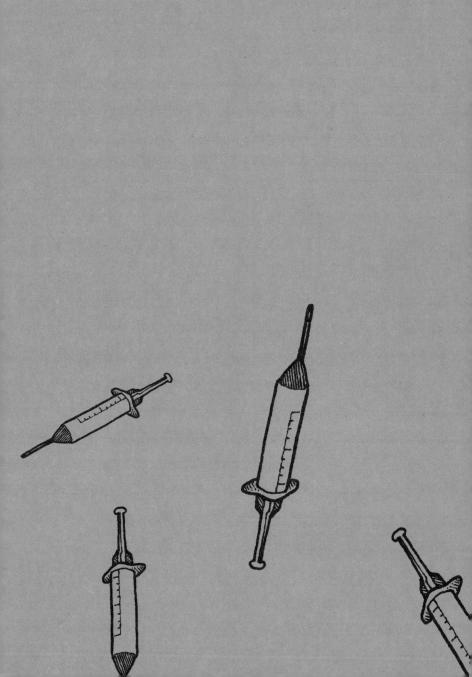

BREAK A LEG

You don't need a book for this; breaking bones is without a doubt one of those things you need to go to hospital for. Bones aren't meant to be broken, but when they are, they need to be set and sometimes even operated on.

If you are an overachiever and in addition to breaking your bone you've also managed to split your skin open, the biggest priority is to stop any bleeding. You can do this by riffling through your fully stocked first-aid kit to find clean cloth bandages, then using them to apply pressure to the wound. Keep whatever you've broken still to stop yourself from doing any more damage, 'cause let's face it, it's pretty likely that you'll fall over and break the other arm too.

One in three women over the age of 50 will experience a bone fracture related to osteoporosis. Welcome to adult life.

If you're capable, or have friends (unlikely…), splint the limb. This doesn't have to be done with anything in particular; a very wise MacGyver-esque friend of mine once splinted a broken arm with an empty case of VB and a roll of duct tape (not recommended, but impressive nonetheless). Once you've fashioned your splint, use icepacks to prevent further swelling and pain until you can get to a hospital. Please keep in mind that a splint should not be used in lieu of medical attention.

I don't know how many times I need to say it, but you're not a doctor; stop disappointing your parents and visit the professionals.

Nicotine use slows down your body's ability to heal. Breaking a bone is as good a reason as any to give up the death-sticks. Remember, smokers are jokers.

Shit you should know

Depending on the severity of the break, you may go into shock. So, lie back, chill out, and try not to focus on how you've just broken an essential part of your body. Look on the bright side: everyone loves to sign a cast!

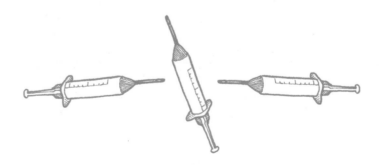

PRETENDING
YOU'RE NOT A
LAZY SHIT

IT'S A WIDELY accepted fact that fitness and strength make us live longer and better. Unfortunately, they also make us want to die… When it comes down to it, there's a metric shit-ton of information floating around about exercise, dieting, supplements and everything else you never really wanted to know about your body and how to make it look less like a flesh-coloured beanbag. Frankly, it's overwhelming – I know, because I did all the sad and depressing research to save you from being crushed under a pile of information. You're bloody welcome! Feast on the fruits of my sweaty labours while I go and eat a donut.

MAKING A PLAN TO MAKE A PLAN TO WORK OUT

If you haven't realised by now, a significant portion of adulting is dedicated to making plans. It's almost impossible to be a successful adult without having some semblance of a plan, so with that in mind, I am constructing a plan to plan my life – starting with fitness.

Fitness is one of those things that doesn't have a one-size-fits-all model. Sure, there are the basics: exercise is good for you; binge drinking and subsisting on a diet of pizza and Froot Loops, not so much. But when it comes to making a fitness plan that you're going to enjoy, stick to and see results from, the key is developing something orientated around your goals and interests. Before you put together a routine, ask yourself these questions:

* **What are** your goals?
* **What kind of** exercise do you like doing? It's okay, nobody *actually* likes to run; that's an urban legend, like buying a property in Sydney and Donald Trump's hair.
* **How long** can you dedicate to exercise? Like, actually how long? Don't say you're going to work out for an hour, five days a week, if all you're capable of is a walk to the fridge three times a night.
* **Do you have** any injuries? Make sure you factor any limitations into your plan. Be realistic.

VARIETY IS THE SPICE OF LIFE

If you're still interested in fitness and not crying in the corner over your own inadequacies after this self-assessment, it's time to make a plan. Like so many things in life, the best plans are often the simplest. A good weight-training plan should target five main areas, varying between a mix of these exercises for each.

* **Quads:** Squats, lunges and box jumps.
* **Butt and hamstrings:** Glute bridges, deadlifts, lunges, squats and step-ups are all essential components to building that glorious peach-butt you've always dreamed of.
* **Chest, shoulders and triceps:** Overhead presses, bench presses, incline dumbbell presses, push-ups and dips – basically all those oh-so-painful and sadly functional push movements.
* **Back, biceps and forearms:** Chin-ups, pull-ups, bodyweight and dumbbell rows – these are the pull to the push of the chest, shoulders and triceps.
* **Core:** Planks, side planks, crunches and mountain climbers.

Add to the work-out burn by focusing on these five areas and rotating your exercises through the week to keep your body guessing. Once you're starting to feel comfortable with your plan, develop a new regime that targets the same areas.

WHEN WILL IT END?!

Once you've figured out what exercises you're actually going to do, you need to determine how long you're going to do them for. Reps and sets form the base timing of any work-out. A 'rep' is the number of times you repeat an exercise, and a 'set' is a group of consecutive reps. Again, the structure of your sets and reps should be determined by your goal.

* **Sets:** A good aim is 3–5 sets per exercise, not including 1–2 warm-up sets with a lighter weight. If you're unsure where to start, try for 4 and go from there. If your arms

fall off halfway through, you've gone too hard.

∗ **Reps:** While sets are important, reps are where you can really tailor your plan to your work-out goals.
  - Building muscle density: 1–5 reps per set
  - Building equal muscular strength to size: 6–12 reps per set
  - Building muscular endurance: 12+ reps

This is just the basis of setting up a fitness plan. Without knowing specific goals and physiology, it can be hard to build something that's more than a generic idea of what a plan should look like. In saying that, once you've factored in all your personal information, there are a few things that can keep you on track.

∗ **Have realistic goals,** with smaller milestones along the way to keep yourself motivated.

∗ **Your brain is unreliable.** Write everything down to keep track of your progress.

∗ **Warm up** before you start, and stretch out when you're done. There are few things in life worse than severe DOMS – Delayed Onset Muscle Soreness (I'm a fitness guru now, I have to use the lingo) – and tearing your groin because you haven't stretched enough is one of them. I speak from painful experience…

RUNNING IS THE DEVIL

If a killer muscular work-out plan isn't enough for you, and you feel the need to torture yourself further, it's time to learn to run. It's an accepted scientific fact that running is the sport of Satan (sweating is just a socially acceptable version of exorcism). By this point, humans really should have evolved past the point of using their legs at all, so why would anyone take up this heinous and unpleasant sport? Well, to show that they're better, fitter and more pretentious than everyone else, obviously…

If you're ready to show the world you're a beacon of fitness – and give yourself a good reason to wear activewear in public – the first thing you need to learn is form. When you're running, both the pavement and your body take a real pounding. To avoid absolutely decimating your joints, and a slew of lewd and obscene jokes about the word 'pounding', keep these words of wisdom in mind.

* **Look straight ahead**, not just for form purposes, but because exercise is less beneficial if you kill yourself running headfirst into oncoming traffic.
* **Don't hunch your shoulders**: keep your chest out and proud, and shoulders back.
* **Lead with your hips**, almost like there's a leash around your waist and it's pulling you far from a world where you ever have to run again.
* **Keep your hands relaxed** and your arms at 90 degrees. Try to move them back and forward in motion with your stride, not across your body – this does nothing and makes you look like more of an idiot than usual.
* **Land with a slight bend** in your knee: this helps absorb some of the impact and takes pressure off your old and deteriorating joints.

* **Try to keep** your steps short and light: your run should be light and quiet, not like a parade of clowns slapping their giant shoes along the pavement.
* **Breathe deeply** and rhythmically, and try to time your movement with your breath. This will also give you something else to focus on instead of the immense physical pain you're in.

If you're just starting out and struggling to see how running could ever be anything more than a 4-minute sprint followed by 40 minutes of 'I'm going to vomit and pass out on the grass', an easy way to train is the 'run–walk–run' method. This ingeniously named practice was developed by Olympian Jeff Galloway, so you know it's gonna be good. The run–walk–run method consists of running, followed by walking. I know, shocker, right? Start by running for 30 seconds, followed by 1–2 minutes of brisk walking, then repeat. The more confident you get, the longer you can extend your running time.

THE RUN—DOWN

When getting into the stride of things, use a simple training plan to stay on track.

* *Train 3 times a week.*
* *Run, or run–walk–run, for 20–30 minutes at least 2 days a week.*
* *On the weekends, go for a slightly longer run.*
* *Either rest or do some form of alternate training on your off-days. Anything where you're strengthening your glutes and legs will help you with long-term running endurance.*
* *Try to keep your runs at a relaxed pace, where you could hold a conversation if you actually had a friend to run with – you're running, not sprinting.*
* *Do a dynamic warm-up before your runs, NOT stretching. A dynamic warm-up consists of movements that prepare your body for the horrors it's about to endure. Walking lunges, leg swings, high knees and butt kicks will help get your muscles working. Stretching, on the other hand, will loosen everything up and make you more prone to injury. Not ideal before you take a pounding.*
* *Start slow and focus on form.*
* *Try running up some hills: this will force you to shorten your stride and be more controlled in your movements. Please note, this will not be pleasant; if I were you, I'd give up now.*
* *Cool down after your run by jogging slowly, but don't stop altogether.*
* *Find pretty places to run, and vary the location. This will both keep you motivated and help give you some multi-terrain experience, not to mention a great background for the candid running shots you'll share with your pretentious running posse.*

EXERCISES WITH UP

Luckily for us all, those famous 'up' movements are not only the cornerstone of the #fitlife, but also way cheaper than a gym membership.

PUSH-UPS

I'm a millennial, and a lazy one at that. With my severe shortcomings in mind, I want an exercise that's simple and efficient – and that exercise is the simple push-up. Push-ups target a lot of important upper-body shit, including:

* **Pectoral** muscles
* **Shoulders** (deltoids, if you're feeling fancy)
* **Triceps**
* **Abdominals**
* **'Wing' muscles**, aka *latissimus dorsi*

Before you get fancy, master the basics.

* Start in the plank position, with your palms directly under your shoulders.
* Brace your core and keep your back straight.
* Keeping your core engaged, lower your body by bending your elbows, keeping them slightly pointed back. Lower yourself until your chest hits the floor – if this is your first time, you'll probably have to live on the floor from now on; if that's too difficult, lower yourself until you feel like your arms are going to fall off.
* Extend your elbows and push your body back to starting position, then begin the torture again.
* Think about your push-up like a moving plank: all the difficulty of an ab exercise, with some extra arm action thrown in.

Push-ups are super versatile and, at the risk of sounding like an infomercial, they're also simple and free – the two key requirements for all the best things.

SIT–UPS

Let's crush an exercise myth here and now: you cannot spot-target fat. Believe me, no one was more depressed than me to find out you can't just do a million sit-ups to annihilate that little belly bulge, but sadly it's true. While doing a shitload of sit-ups won't target your belly fat, it will strengthen your abdominals, not to mention your chest, hip flexors and lower back.

Like push-ups, sit-ups are one of those glorious exercises that are basic and free!

* Lie on your back with your knees bent and feet firmly on the ground; this will anchor you to the ground.
* Avoid the awkward 'What do I do with my hands?' freak-out by putting them behind your ears or cross your arms and place your hands on opposite shoulders.
* Without pulling or straining your neck, curl your upper body up towards your knees, letting everyone in the gym know you're working hard by exhaling loudly as you go.
* Slowly lower yourself back to the ground, letting your spine lengthen along the floor as you inhale.

In recent years there's been some debate about whether sit-ups do more harm than good. If you lose focus on your form (as with any exercise) you're risking a lower-back or neck injury. Make sure to perform, not only this, but every exercise, deliberately and with focus to protect your sad, aging body from injury.

WHERE PEACH-BUTTS ARE MADE

While working out can be a real pain in the arse, the sweaty, juicy peach-butt rewards are well worth it. One of the best ways to grow a butt that can really be ap-peach-iated is through exercise. A consistent routine with at least three targeted work-outs a week is the ultimate path to backing up those butt-gains.

SQUATS

Squats are probably one of the best types of strength exercise. There are about a million different ways to do them, suited to any goals, restrictions or fitness levels. As with many weighted exercises, form is one of the most important aspects of squatting; it's essential to be slow and controlled in your movement, and if something hurts, stop.

Peaches: a delicious fruit and the butt of every joke. Building a peach-butt is definitely a trend I can get behind.

PLEASE NOTE: The gym is not the club. Don't poke your butt out and dip your back; keep everything tight and controlled, and your back should be straight while doing this movement.

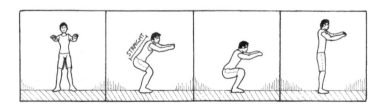

For a standard squat:

1   **Stand tall** with your feet slightly further than hip-width apart, toes pointed outwards at a 30–35 degree angle.

2   **Keep your back straight** as you drive your hips back, bending at the knee and ankles and pressing your knees slightly outwards.

3   **Sit into the squat**, going as deeply as you can.

4   **Keep your feet glued** to the ground as you straighten back up.

CLAMSHELLS

Most of the exercises that give you a butt worth staring at are ones you never want to be seen doing in public… Clamshells target your gluteus maximus and medius: the outside of your hip and bum.

1   **Lie on your side** with your legs stacked and lift your top leg 90 degrees while your bottom leg stays pressed to the ground.

2   **Lower your top leg** down and completely relax at the end of the movement.

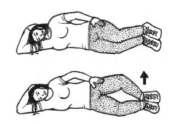

3   **Repeat** on the opposite side.

BUILD A BRIDGE (WITH YOUR BUTT)

Glute bridges work your glutes, hamstrings, back and abdominals – areas that perfectly frame your growing peach, emphasising all its muscular glory.

1   **Lie face up** with your feet about 30 centimetres from the glorious booty.

2   **Squeeze your butt** and lift your lower back from the ground, forming a straight line with your body, and keeping your arms on the ground with your palms facing down.

3   **Lower back** to the ground – try to make this lowering motion last about 4 seconds.

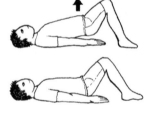

4   **Avoid making** awkward eye contact with anyone else in the gym, and repeat.

LUNGES

Lunges are basically fancy walking. This is another exercise that has seemingly endless variations and benefits. Lunges strengthen your glutes, quads and hamstrings, and provide a foundation for the perfect power pose.

1   **Think of your legs** as railway tracks and stand with your feet hip-width apart.

2.   **Lunge back** with your right foot for a reverse lunge, bending both knees as you go.

3   **Bring your foot back** to starting position and complete the motion again, alternating legs.

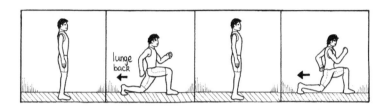

DEADLIFTS

The final link in the fantastic-butt chain. When done with correct form, deadlifts are a great exercise to add to your routine, not just for that Greek-god-like posterior, but also for core, lower back and abdominals. Again, this is another exercise that comes with a million variations, all of which target slightly different areas. The Romanian deadlift is one of the most popular versions and is sure to initiate you into that squat-rack crew with all the other beefcakes.

PLEASE NOTE: While deadlifts have an amazing array of benefits, they can really fuck you up if you don't know what you're doing. Before you start lifting, it's insanely important to be aware of your form, ESPECIALLY if you're using heavy weights. Oddly enough, backs are pretty important, and slipping a disk is an experience you should leave until your late sixties – at least.

1   **Hold the bar** at hip height with a pronated grip (that's a fancy way of telling you to have your palms facing towards you).

2   **Pull your shoulders** back with your chest out proud and bend your knees slightly.

3   **Lower the bar** by moving that peach of an arse back, pushing back through your hips as far as you can. Thinking of your hips as a giant human hinge is an easy way to focus on form in this movement. Keep your back flat and core engaged as you lower the weight.

4   **Keep the bar** close to your body, head forward and shoulders back. You should be able to reach just below your knees.

5   **Thrust forward** with your hips to return to an upright position, making sure to keep your core tight and back strong – remember, control is key here: no jerky movements.

Shit you should know

There's a sad little fact about our bodies that exercise only accounts for 20% of your gains or losses. 80% of your results are driven by diet. The upside of this is that if you're trying to grow your butt into a delicious juicy peach, then you're growing muscle, and muscles need to eat.

To lose weight, your body needs to be in a calorie deficit, but to gain muscle you need to be in a surplus. Protein is a really important aspect of muscle building. When our bodies digest protein, it breaks down into amino acids, which are important for a whole range of bodily functions, not just muscle development. Foods like eggs, nuts, fish, chicken, steak and chickpeas are packed full of protein.

HIIT: HATING INTENSIVE INVOLUNTARY TORTURE

High Intensity Interval Training. Definitely as horrible as it sounds. Recently, HIIT has been made popular and accessible by fitness clubs/cults like CrossFit and F45. These churches of sweat bring you into the gym for 45 minutes to an hour to push you to the point where you want to throw up. HIIT comprises short bursts of exercise alternated with recovery periods. The higher intensity periods create an elevated metabolic demand, while the recovery brings you back down into an aerobic zone. Basically, this means you freak the fuck out of your body, give it a second to rest, and then do it all over again.

If you've ever wished you could drown in a puddle of your own sweat, then HIIT is the exercise for you!

While HIIT is a terrifying test of your fitness, it has a whole bunch of health benefits.

* **Helps shed body fat** – the more intense the exercise, the more fat burn.
* **Strengthens** the cardiovascular system.
* **Develops** endurance.
* **Gives Insta-worthy toning** and definition, because what's the point of exercising if you can't tell everyone about it on social media, right?
* **Fast and effective** training.

While you can venture out into the world of fitness cults to get help assaulting your body with a barrage of HIIT exercises, there are a few templates and guidelines you can use to work out in the privacy of your own home so hard you want to vomit.

TABATA

This is the most common HIIT template. The structure of Tabata sessions are 20 seconds on and 10 seconds off, with a total of 8 intervals per exercise – you can basically choose whatever exercises you'd like to incorporate into these sessions and torture yourself with as many repetitions as you're physically capable of. While these lightning-quick sets may sound like an easy way to decimate your body fat, I'm going to have to crush all your hopes and dreams and remind you that a key component of HIIT is the HIGH INTENSITY of these work-outs. If you spend 50% of your session fucking around with your weights, slowly prepping yourself to start a set, and not really giving it your all, you might as well not bother.

1:2 RATIO

If you're struggling to understand how to format your own private sessions of suffering, the 1:2 ratio is a good rule of thumb. Pick an exercise, do it for 30, 60 or 90 seconds, and then recover for twice as long. As soon as your endurance starts to improve and you no longer feel like you're going to die halfway through your work-out, you can transition to a 1:1 ratio and begin the torture cycle all over again.

TIMING

HIIT sessions generally last around 20–45 minutes. As a rule, you want a good work-out (not just HIIT) to go for about 45 minutes. F45 has very successfully adapted this rule to their ever so creatively named 'Functional 45' cult.

PRO TIPS:

A few other things to keep in mind when diving into the sweaty, painful world of HIIT are:

* **Recovery is key** to a successful HIIT session. When you recover, you're helping build your cardio conditioning, which will increase your endurance over time. Not to mention, resting between reps will allow you to go harder when you're actually working out.

* **Technique is so important**. When you're doing a normal, steady-paced work-out, you have plenty of time to perfect your form and take it slow. In a HIIT work-out everything is going a million miles a minute, and when you're squatting 40 kilos with a clock ticking down behind you, it's easy to forget your form and fuck yourself over. Make the most of the work-out time, but always focus on technique. HIIT may give you the body you want, but you won't be able to use it if you've busted a hip and you're walking around like a wasted geriatric.

* **Keep your heart rate up**. Like I said, HIIT is about high intensity. While those rest sets are important, it doesn't mean anything if you aren't pushing yourself as hard as you can when you're moving.

* **You're going to be sweaty** – so sweaty you might think you're going to drown in a pool of your own bodily fluids. Bring a towel.

HIIT is an expensive, modern-day equivalent of whipping your body until you can't move anymore. Treat yourself nicely and prepare. Warm up before you begin and stretch when you're done. Make friends with the foam roller – that baby is going to be your saving grace.

MOBILITY, FLEXIBILITY AND STRENGTH: MOVE FREELY, STUPID

These three cornerstones of fitness are often seen as interchangeable – however, just like you (what a surprise), they are all special little snowflakes, so need to be treated as such.

MOBILITY

The definition of mobility is the ability to move freely and easily, but in a more technical sense, mobility is having strength and control in your range of motion.

Mobility is important for overall injury prevention; it makes sense that the more strength and control you have, the less likely you are to damage yourself while using your body. Sadly, humans are like giant soft peaches in that we're easily bruised and very delicious. Where we differ is that we're also prone to doing heinously stupid things. Being mobile can reduce the risk of those stupid things damaging you so badly you'll never have the chance to do them again.

There are a few things you can do to develop your mobility.

* **Foam rolling**: I cannot recommend this enough. The pleasure/pain you'll get from that little cylinder of foam is not to be scoffed at. It's a love–hate relationship that should not be taken for granted.
* **Use your body**: I know, right? WILD. Using your body and taking it through a full range of motion 1–2 times a week will help keep everything nice and limber. Make sure to maintain control of your body as you use it, swinging and jerking yourself around is just going to break something, most likely your dignity…

FLEXIBILITY

Flexibility is all about the length of your muscles and the range of motion your joints can achieve, as opposed to mobility, which is the ability to move without restriction. They sound like basically the same thing, but I promise they're not!

Flexibility is great for more than just putting your legs behind your head, and will help with:

* **Reduced soreness** post-exercise.
* **Using less energy** while in motion, hence improving your overall performance. #athlete
* **Improving your posture** – now people will no longer be able to tell how weighed down you are by your own existence.

STRETCHING THE TRUTH

While flexibility is something you should try to focus on evenly throughout your body, some areas are going to be more flexible than others due to your exercise of choice or your weird genetics. Don't stress if you can't ever touch your toes – some people just aren't as gifted as others.

Flexibility will improve naturally the more active you are, but the most efficient way to increase your flexibility is through stretching. Personally, stretching is my favourite part of exercising. It's the reward at the end of a session when all you want to do is collapse in a sobbing mess on the floor.

Stretching is an activity that should be done after your work-out, not before. If done before, it can loosen you out, which in theory sounds good, but in practice can make you floppy, hopeless and generally more likely to sprain or tear something, especially if you're doing a vigorous exercise. That said, warming up with dynamic exercises before you start working out is a helpful way to prep yourself for your oncoming slaughter. Once you're all warm and exhausted, it's time to get started on those stretches.

* **Static stretching:** Find a good stretching position that lengthens whatever muscle you're targeting and hold it for 15–60 seconds. Breathe in deeply as you hold your position.

* **Dynamic stretching:** Pick your stretch and gently move in and out of it, lengthening the muscle. If you want to get fancy, transition into a ballistic stretch by adding a slight and gentle bounce. Note the word 'gentle' – bouncing too hard when stretching can cause microtrauma in your muscles. Microtrauma heals through scar tissue, something which actually tightens your muscles and reduces flexibility, rendering all your hours of stretching wasted.

* **Active Isolated Stretch:** An AIS is another type of dynamic stretching that moves your joints through a full range of motion, holding the stretch at the end-point briefly (the place where you can feel the strongest stretch), before returning to the start of your motion and repeating.

---

* *Stretch your whole body, not just the sore bits. If you only focus on one area, you'll end up disproportionate and weirder than you already are.*
* *Don't bounce in the stretch – that is how you tear things.*
* *Stretch to the point of tension, not pain. Again, tearing things = bad.*

Shit you should know

STRENGTH

Out of mobility, flexibility and strength, strength is the hardest to define because it means a variety of different things to different people. To me, strength means being able to lift my own body weight without dropping myself and eating shit; to others, it means being able to carry groceries in from the car. Set your standards and go from there. Strength plays a pretty massive role in how we perform our daily activities, and unsurprisingly, has a heap of health benefits, including:

The simplest way to think of physical strength is by your ability to overcome a given force.

* **Weight management** – the more muscle mass you have, the more calories you burn through the day.
* **Improved bone density** – muscles, now with extra calcium.
* **Prevention of osteoporosis** – because if adulthood can be characterised by anything, it's the fear of your oncoming physical demise.

Strength is something that needs to be built on, and its potential for growth is massive. Strength training, in theory, is relatively easy, and requires a focus on weight training with heavier weights and less reps. Establishing a fitness plan with your strength goals in mind is the easiest way to develop the level of strength you're after.

AEROBIC VS ANAEROBIC

There are exercises that leave you gasping for breath and wondering how you're still alive, while others make you feel strong and powerful as you glimmer in a sheen of your own bodily fluids. Understanding the difference between the two will not make these torturous activities any easier, but at least you'll know why you're suffering so much.

AEROBIC

Aerobic literally means 'involving oxygen'. This means it's an exercise that requires energy, primarily through oxygenated blood being pumped through your heart and out to all your sad, stressed-out muscles. Running at a reasonable pace with a heart rate of around 130 bpm (beats per minute), swimming, cycling and dancing are all activities that would likely put you in an aerobic zone.

Aerobic exercise is exceptionally good for your body, and while it may not wash away all your sins, such exercises will certainly help you recover from a fair few of them.

* **Improves** your overall health and wellbeing.
* **Burns fat** (i.e. it wipes your body clean of every 2 am halal snack pack you've ever eaten).
* **Improves** your mood (once you've stopped sweating, that is…).
* **Strengthens** your heart and lungs.
* **Reduces** your risk of diabetes and osteoporosis, and lessens your catapult-like approach into old age.

Aerobic exercises performed at a moderate level of activity should be undertaken five times a week for around 30 minutes to get the full sin-cleansing benefits. May your sweat baptise you into a new realm of fitness.

ANAEROBIC

All good things come in pairs, and anaerobic is the gin to the tonic that is aerobic. While aerobic is best buds with oxygen, anaerobic exercise goes without – but that doesn't mean you hold your breath. These exercises are of higher intensity and get you out of breath quickly. When you're performing anaerobic exercises, your body requires more immediate energy and relies on your stored energy, rather than oxygen, for fuel.

Weight lifting, sprinting, climbing stairs, HIIT and basically any aerobic exercise done at a high intensity all fall into an anaerobic category. The benefits of doing this kind of activity include:

* **Building** lean muscle mass.
* **Weight management** (I hope you're seeing the trend here: exercise = fat loss).
* **Helps build** your endurance and fitness levels, so you can stop being embarrassed when you get puffed walking up the stairs.

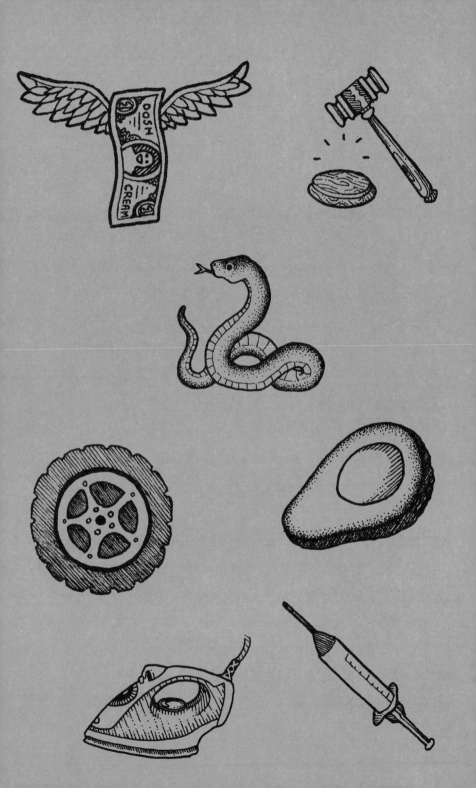

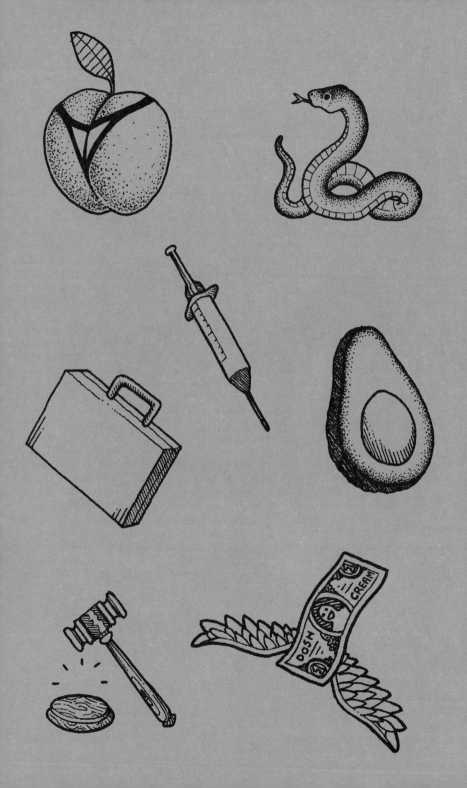

THANK GOD THAT'S OVER

Jokes. It's never really over. The adult world is a difficult and scary place, and if writing this book has taught me anything it's that you need a ridiculous number of skills to keep yourself alive, from real-life shit, like treating burns and performing CPR, to the shockingly basic essentials like making gravy, learning to run and writing a resume. Not to mention the things I never, ever want to think about again, like the millions of light bulbs and their various shapes, how to mend a seam, and the fact that I have been sleeping in my own filthy sheets for so long I've probably become one human-sized bacteria. Adult life is really fucking hard and, to be honest, I'd STILL rather not do it.

No one knows what the fuck is going on, but real adults are great at pretending!

But, if there's one take-home message from this book (aside from how to fold a fitted sheet, because let's be real: that's essentially a magic trick that I've started performing to the amazement of crowds at parties) it's that the key to successful adulting is organisation, overconfidence and swearing. This trifecta of adulthood is the light that shines the way through the terrifying decades of planning and decay to come. Despite still being an absolute trash bag of a person, I now have the knowledge to fake it 'til I make it or die trying… and I hope you do too! I've even got one super-special extra pearl of wisdom for you: it turns out even real adults don't have a clue what they're doing; they're stumbling through life just as lost and confused as we are, they've just had more practice pretending they know what the fuck is going on. Don't let their bravado fool you, we're all in this mess together.

With your new fake-adult knowledge in mind, try not to stress too much. Embrace your age, make some plans, keep learning more shit and grow the fuck up.

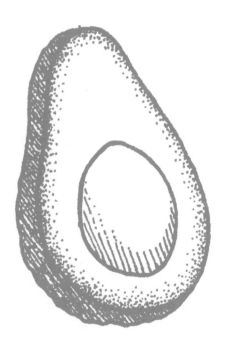

ACKNOWLEDGEMENTS

They say it takes a village to raise a child. As it turns it out, it takes a village to keep a hopeless millennial from dying in a pool of their own tears. My village is ridiculously large and equally amazing and has been instrumental in inspiring and informing both this book and my adult existence.

When I was a tiny non-adult, my biggest dream was to write a book. If it wasn't for the amazing team at Pantera Press that dream would have never come true, so thank you to the incredible, talented and hilarious people who make Pantera such a wonderful place to work.

A massive thank you to Marty and Ali for letting me go wild with this ridiculous idea. Anabel, for all of your support, wisdom, mentorship and everything else – I promise I'll stop hassling you for a launch now. Editor Lucy Bell, thank you for answering my billions of questions, stressing with me and giving me all the editorial guidance and support I so desperately needed. Elly from Work, for making this book so pretty, and for giving me a soundtrack to write to. Thank you, Lex, for all your encouragement and for letting me have a green book! Thank you, James, Lucy, Katy, Jenny, John, Anne and Kirsty!

In the world outside my amazing publishing bubble, an enormous amount of thanks needs to be given to Alex Nicol, the incredible artist responsible for the illustrations that made this book so much cooler than my words ever could!

It's pretty obvious at this point that my knowledge of the world needed some very detailed and patient informing from people who know far more than me. This book would just be a recipe for gravy and a diagram of how to fold a fitted sheet without the wisdom of all these brilliant people who let me interview/badger them for the answers to life's questions in exchange for my eternal gratitude and a mention in the acknowledgements:

* Jenny Green, the finance guru. Money is still my number-one fear, but thanks to you I can pretend I understand what superannuation is.
* Tony Blackie and Jennifer McDonald, small business experts and 10/10 parents. Thanks for answering all my questions, and for teaching me to read and stuff so I could actually write this book.
* Kieran Breen, Tree Man. Thanks for knowing about the outdoors so I never have to go outside.
* Joshua Denning-Peattie, the wise engineer. I'm not sure how many ex-boyfriends would let their exes interview them for a book, but I'm very glad you did!
* John M. Green, expert on the law and general giver of great advice!
* Mary-Anne Yeldham and Hollie Bainbridge, nurses-galore and all-round geniuses. Thank you for all your medical wisdom (and for fixing every ailment and injury I've ever had…).
* Dorothea Mackellar, Paul Kelly and Kanye West for their creative inspiration from 'My Country', 'Gold Digger' and 'How to Make Gravy'. Please don't sue me.

There also has to be special shout-out to all the people who have listened to me talk about this book non-stop for the last year: Tegan, Sean, Joseph, Kieran, Lauren, Holly, Sammy, Pete, Candace, Jemma and James – my collective army of housemates (both past and present), squad and family, who've had to suffer through my stress, endless stupid questions, and secret use of their lack of life knowledge as inspiration. Thanks for generally being the most wonderful humans, and for struggling through this terrible adult life with me.

AUTHOR BIO

Anna Blackie is a real-life hopeless millennial who spends her time advising other millennials on how to function in an attempt to avoid her own shortcomings.

Anna's long-term love of words and inappropriate sniffing of old books led her into a Bachelor of Arts majoring in English and Writing at Macquarie University. After that, she decided three years of full-time reading just weren't enough and went into publishing, where she now works in the editorial department of a fun, fresh, up-and-coming Australian publishing house.

While living in Sydney and dreaming of one day eating an avocado in her very own house, Anna realised there was a shocking amount she didn't know about how to function in the adult world. In a blind-leading-the-blind situation, she decided to write her very own guide to being a grown-up, *How to Adult*, and fill it with all the things she hoped she would one day understand.